W9-DJM-947

CONCILIUM

Religion in the Seventies

CONCILIUM

Concilium October, 1977: Ecumenism

WHY DID GOD MAKE ME?

Edited by

Hans Küng and
Jürgen Moltmann

A CROSSROAD BOOK

The Seabury Press • New York

1978
The Seabury Press
815 Second Avenue
New York, N.Y. 10017

Library of Congress Catalog Card Number: 78-51439
ISBN: 0-8164-0366-X
ISBN: 0-8164-2167-6 (pbk.)

CONTENTS

Part III
Suggestions for a New Answer

Part IV
Assessment and Synthesis

PART I

Why Did God Make Me? Basic Issues

Hans Küng

The Problem of the Catechism Question: 'Why are we on earth?'— 'Why did God make me?'

AT A public press conference given by *Concilium* theologians on the subject of 'the Position of Christianity', held in Munich in 1975, a journalist asked: 'Does the question of the old catechism still hold good today?' The question and answer to which the journalist referred are:

> Why are we on earth?—We are on earth to know God, love him and serve him and in this way get to heaven.

AN ECUMENICAL TASK

This question is at the beginning of all the traditional Catholic catechisms. The question and answer quoted above are based on the formula of Joseph Leharpe, S.J., and dates back to 1847. In other languages, the formula of Cardinal Pietro Gasparri's *Catechismus Catholicus* of 1930 is more often used:

> Why did God make you?—God made me to know him, love him and keep his commandments and in this way to be blessed in heaven after death.

This is, then, a typically Catholic question. It is , however, also asked in the catechisms of other churches, although it often occurs in a different place, in a different form and with a different answer. As an exam-

3

ple of this, we can quote the similar formula in Calvin's Geneva Catechism of 1542, which appears at the very beginning of the section 'On the Articles of Faith':

> 1. *Le ministre: Quelle est la principale fin de la vie humaine? L'enfant: C'est de congnoistre Dieu.* (What is the chief end of human life?—To know God.)
> 2. *Pourquoy dis-tu cela? Pource qu'il nous a créé et mis au monde pour estre glorifié en nous. Et c'est bien raison, que nous rapportions nostre vie á sa gloire: puis qu'il en est le commancement.* (Why do you say that?—Because he created us and put us in the world to be glorified in us. And we do indeed ascribe our life to his glory, for he is its origin.)

This catechism question is clearly a question about the meaning of life and every Church is bound to seek an answer to it, in catechisms or elsewhere, and in this form or another. The investigation of the various confessional answers to this question within the framework of theology can be conducted ecumenically.

If the task is to be carried out correctly, three conditions must be fulfilled. Firstly, prominence must be given to the positive kerygmatic, catechetical and pastoral intentions of the traditional confessional formulae. Secondly, both the question and the answer have to be tested against their conformity with the biblical message and their intelligibility in the modern world and contemporary society. Thirdly, we must try to find an answer to this catechism question which is both amplified and corrected and therefore more all-embracing and profound, and which can at the same time be understood, not only in each individual confession, but in an ecumenical context.

The old formula, then, should not simply be discarded, nor should it be repeated in exactly the same form. On critical examination, the old answer should prove to be neither senseless nor eternal and beyond time, but rather historically and socially conditioned and therefore in need of constant renewal. It is not a question of the constancy of the terminology and concepts used. What we have to consider is rather the *constancy of the great intentions and the decisive content.* Nothing should be taken away from the truth of the old formula as covered by Scripture. This truth ought rather to be brought more clearly to light if it is transferred from the socio-cultural context in which the old question and answer were formulated to the context of the modern world. It will, moreover, not be necessary to find an ecumenical *formula* that is common to all the Churches—many different emphases are possible that relate specifically to particular confessions or cultures. There should, however, be agreement among Christians with regard to their common *faith* in a Christian meaning of life. This shared faith will therefore be expressed in different formulae.

As usual, the writing of the articles for this number of *Concilium* was preceded by consultation on the part of the members of the editorial committee of the journal itself and those of the sectional committee dealing with Ecumenism. It was consequently decided that two perspectives should be constantly present in this ecumenical task and at least borne in mind in this introductory article.

The first perspective is that there is considerable competition provided by other, non-Christian answers to the question about the meaning of life. Answers are given both by the secular ideologies and by the great world religions.

There are also other perspectives in Scripture and the Christian tradition which are not expressed, or insufficiently expressed, in the traditional catechism answers provided by the various Christian confessions.

NON-CHRISTIAN ANSWERS TO BE CONSIDERED

We do not need to spend long in discussion to know that the question 'Why are we on earth?' is answered as materialistically and often more banally in the democratic West as it is in the Communist East. There are, of course, very many major or minor *secular ideologies*, seeking to explain the meaning of life, in the *West*. For each individual, this meaning of life is often an individually mixed 'cocktail', made up of many different ingredients, each offering a meaning. This meaning of life is reflected to a greater or lesser extent in the professional sphere, the career structure and work and possessions generally, as well as in the striving for a better and better standard of living. All this can, of course, be expressed a little more idealistically: the meaning of life is found in the widespread desire for self-realization, universal humanization and the greatest possible development of the individual in a correspondingly changed society. Questions have certainly been asked by the younger generation, at least since the period of student unrest, whether all this is really sufficient as an aim in life; whether a higher standard of living can replace a meaning of life; and whether, finally, there is not an urgent need for new ideals, models and norms, a new inspiration, a new definition of values and priorities, a new aim in life and indeed a totally new meaning of life.

In the *East* too, Marxist-Leninist materialists are beginning to discuss in a variety of ways questions about meaning, guilt and death in the lives of individual men. The current, orthodox answers of Marxism are well-known—the meaning and fulfilment of life are to be found in work, militant class solidarity, life led in dialogue and the abolition of alienation by socialist society. These current answers, however, cannot silence the 'private' questions of progressive Marxists (in the West as well as in the East) and countless other, unknown people. What are we to think of guilt, suffering and death and the personal destiny of the individual?—they are asking. What is the meaning of life for the individual in the context of the socialist society that has not yet been realized in the sense in which it was outlined by Karl Marx? Should the nation perhaps constitute the ultimate meaning of life, to which everything should be subordinated and, if necessary, sacrificed, as it was in the past in Europe and is now in North America and the Third World? Should we think of nationalism rather than socialism as a quasi-religion?

In the sphere of *science*, too, where the question about the meaning of life has often been suppressed, both in the West and the East, and regarded as a substitute for religion, there is a good deal of new thinking. Natural scientists and those who specialize in the humanities are more aware now of the inadequacy of the materialistic and positivistic understanding of reality. They are beginning to make relative rather than absolute claims for their own scientific method and to be more open to other questions beyond the scope of science. Many of them recognize clearly that responsible scientific and technical activity necessarily implies ethics, and ethics in turn implies a scale of values, guidelines and the quest for meaning. Psychologists—and especially those specializing in depth psychology—have above all discovered the extreme importance of the whole question of the meaning of life for the human psyche, its consciousness and its cure. Contemporary psychoanalysts have pointed to an important connection between the decline of religiosity and the increase in loss of direction, norms and meaning—ills that are as characteristic of our own time as sexual neuroses were at the time of Victorian prudery when Sigmund Freud was practising his skills.

Since this question about the meaning of life is, however, being asked even by those whose ideologies are secular, their positive concern for a deeper definition of the Christian interpretation of the meaning of life must be taken more seriously. Ought we Christians, in other words, not to consider more fully than we have in the past the other perspectives in the traditional catechism answer: 'to serve God and in this way get to heaven'? That is, not only God and the divine, but man and everything that is human? Not only heaven, but earth, life on earth and the things of this earth? Not only 'know God, love him and serve him' but concern ourselves deeply with man and his development and humanization? Here and now? Ought we not also to think more clearly now than we have in the past about the ultimate aim of man's daily work, the individual's inclusion in the collective reality and social relationships and the abolition of alienation, and authentic emancipation?

In addition to taking the questions and answers of the secular ideologies seriously, we must also consider very carefully those provided by the great *world religions*, which are becoming more and more influential in Europe, America and Africa. Let us very briefly review their answers here.

What is the *Hindu's* aim in life? Through prosperity, pleasure, love and the fulfilment of his ethical and religious duties, he strives to attain a happy life and hopes to be reborn to a better one. Eventually, through many different forms of asceticism and meditation, he looks forward to release from the cycle of rebirth and hopes to leave the deceptive world of appearances (*maya*) and penetrate to the eternal, unchangeable and absolute Brahma, by entering himself.

What is the *Buddhist's* aim in life? By following the 'middle way' between sensual pleasure and ascetic self-mortification and the 'eightfold path' of the Buddha (right seeing and right wanting, right speaking and right doing, right living and right striving, right remembering and right sinking into oneself), he seeks to know the cause of all suffering and repeated rebirths (self-seeking and the thirst for life) and in this way to overcome the suffering itself. His aim, then, is release through gaining insight into the void and consciously not collecting positive and negative data of life (*karma*) and freedom from the endless cycle of rebirth into the world of appearances through being extinguished in the infinite (*nirvana*).

What is the *Muslim's* aim in life? He believes in the one God and his one prophet and submits himself ('Islam') to God's will throughout his whole life. He also regards suffering as God's unchangeable will. In addition to confessing his faith, he has above all the duty to pray daily, give alms, fast during the month of Ramadan and make the pilgrimage to Mecca. (These are the 'five pillars' of Islam.) The aim of this belief and practice is to reach a paradise full of terrestrial delights.

The great world religions, then, also point to a positive need for a better definition of the Christian answer to the question about the meaning of life. For example, we Christians must take much more seriously the original and fundamental experience and hope of the religions that began in India, especially Hinduism and Buddhism, that life implies suffering and new life new suffering and that it is possible to overcome suffering and achieve release and freedom? The original and fundamental experience and hope expressed in these religions may well be a warning to the rather superficial European and American humanists who only take into consideration what is true, good and beautiful in their definition of the meaning of life.

I have indicated a few themes that should be considered more carefully by the Christian tradition and would now like to point briefly to certain Christian perspectives.

CHRISTIAN PERSPECTIVES TO BE CONSIDERED

Various desiderata emerged from the consultation of the committee members and these are well worth taking into consideration. Yves Congar drew our attention to three important points of view. He was of the opinion that the classical answer was true, but incomplete. It was formulated in a spiritual climate and a language that were no longer acceptable to men today. What is lacking in the classical catechism answer, Congar and other theologians thought, is:

1. A social dimension, within which consideration is given not only to humanity, in the sense of the history of mankind, but also to the concrete individual, our fellow man in the small community, and his significance for the meaning of life. We must, in other words, overcome a false individualism in faith.

2. An emphasis on our historical task here on earth. We have, therefore, to try to eliminate a dualism that is not Christian.

3. A Christological orientation. We must correct an un-critical 'natural theology'.

I have already discussed briefly the concern of the secular ideologies and that of the great world religions for a redefinition of the *Christian meaning* of life. I must now indicate the specifically Christian need. Christians ought to consider again today the meaning of Christ for their lives, in the following three areas especially:

1. Jesus Christ makes a *new attitude* or orientation towards life possible and communicates that attitude to man. Man (both individually and collectively) can live more humanly and authentically if his model for life and his relationship with his fellow-men, God and the world is Jesus Christ, who makes it possible for him to have identity and inner coherence in his life.

2. Jesus Christ makes new *motives, actions and dispositions* possible and communicates these to man. Through Jesus Christ, man's disposition can be one of total commitment to his fellow-men, without making any claim for himself, solidarity with the underprivileged and militant opposition to unjust structures. He can also be disposed to thankfulness, freedom, magnanimity, selflessness, joy, forgiveness and service. These dispositions will, with Christ, prove their worth in marginal situations, a readiness to suffer from the fullness of self-giving, renun-

ciation when it is not strictly necessary and a willingness to commit oneself to a greater cause.

3. Jesus Christ makes a new sphere of meaning and a new aim possible and communicates these to man. This new meaning and aim in life are found in the ultimate reality—the fulfilment of man, both individually and collectively, in the kingdom of God. Not only the positive, but the negative aspects of human life can be sustained by this Christian meaning and aim in life. An ultimate meaning is offered, in the light and power of Jesus Christ, not only for life and action, but also for suffering and death and not only for the history of mankind's success, but also for that of his failure and suffering.

This view of the specifically Christian concern helps us to avoid not only the frequently criticized moralism that overlooks the fact that we are given a good life, but also the form of theism that enthrones God above or outside the life of the individual and the history of mankind. What I have said here, however, should not lead the reader to prejudge what follows. My aim has been simply to draw attention to various implications of the theme under discussion and, wherever possible, to stimulate a rethinking of the traditional catechism answer.

Translated by David Smith

Frans van de Poel

'Why Did God Make Me?'—Answers from the Catechism

WHEN I have learnt something as a child, especially when I know that my father learnt it in the same way, I think it has always been like that. In the case of the question in the catechism 'Why did God make you?' I still feel myself inclined to assume rather rashly that this is a matter of a centuries-old tradition. In fact, however, the question is neither that old, nor that universal.

VOICES FROM THE REFORMATION

In Martin Luther's short catechism (1529) we find the floowing text in connection with this first article of faith: 'I believe that God has created me as all other creatures, has given me a body and a soul, eyes, ears and all my limbs, intelligence and all the senses, and preserved me, in view of which he richly and daily provides me with clothes and footwear, food and drink, a house and ground, a wife and child, fields, cattle and all goods, with all the necessaries and livelihood for this body and this life, protects me against all danger and keeps and preserves me from all evil, and does all this out of sheer fatherly and divine goodness and compassion without any merit or worth of my own, for all of which I owe him gratitude and praise, service and obedience; this is undoubt-edly true'.[1] Particularly the last part of this text gives some indication of the purpose of our existence, but it is only seen as a response to what we have received from God.

John Calvin definitely put the question about the purpose of man's existence. His catechism, which was adopted in 1545 in Geneva, opens with the following dialogue:

Minister: Which is the main purpose of man's life?

Child: To know God.

M.: Why do you say that?

C.: Because he has created us and put us in this world in order to be glorified in us. And it is right that we should relate our life to his glory since he is at the origin of it.

M.: And what is the supreme good of man?

C.: The very same.

M.: But when do we truly and rightly know God?

C.: When one knows him, in order to honour him.

M.: How do we honour him properly?

C.: When we put all our trust in him; when we serve him by obedience to his will; when we call on him in all our needs, looking for our salvation and all good things in him, and when we recognize in our heart and in our words that all that is good comes from him alone.[2]

The starting-point is God and his honour, and that is also the sole end. It is perhaps good to add what he says about the resurrection of the body: 'Why is this mentioned in the confession of faith? To warn us that our happiness does not lie on this earth.' It is hardly possible to be more aloof from present realities.

In the *Heidelberger Katechismus* (1563) 'our' question is once again not put explicitly. Yet, it is perhaps interesting to quote the first two questions because we find there the same trend as in Calvin. From this point of view the way the questions are put is already very significant.

1st question: What is your sole consolation in life and death?

Answer: That with my body and soul I belong in life and death not to myself but to my dear saviour Jesus Christ who with his costly blood has fully paid for all my sins and has freed me from all the power of the devil and thus ensures that no hair will fall from my head without the will of my Father in heaven and indeed everything must contribute to my salvation. Also because through his holy Spirit he assures me of life eternal and makes me willing and ready henceforth to live with all my heart.

2nd question: How many things do you have to know so that you can happily live and die in this consoling thought?

Answer: Three things. First how great my sins and misery are. Secondly how I am redeemed from all my sins and misery. And thirdly how I must thank God for this redemption.[3]

I would also briefly refer to the sixth question because the end of the answer to it will return in many other texts with slight modifications:

6th question: Has God then created man in a state of evil and perversity? Answer: No: but God has created man as good and in his own likeness, i.e., in true righteousness and holiness in order that he should know his Creator in truth, love him with all his heart, and live with him in everlasting bliss, praising and glorifying him.[4]

The question appears again, in very explicit form, and again as the first question in the *Emdener Katechismus* (1554).

Question: Why have you been created as man?

Answer: So that I should be an image of God and should know, praise and serve my God and Creator.[5]

So far, some important voices from the Reformation. What was the situation on this point among Catholics at this time: Did they ask themselves the question at all?

THE COUNTER-REFORMATION

Neither in his large catechism of 1554, nor in the small one of 1561 does Canisius deal with the issue as it concerns us here.

In the *Catechismus Romanus* (1568), commissioned by Pius V for the use of priests, we only find the explanation of the creation of heaven and earth: 'And there was no other cause which might impel Him to create than to impart His goodness to what He Himself had brought about.[6] So here the purpose of creation is approached from God's angle, and then more as a gift than as a mandate.

At the request of Clement VIII, Robert Bellarmine, a confrère of Canisius, composed his catechism which appeared in 1598 and remained dominant in the Latin countries until the publication of the catechism of Pius X. But there, too, the matter of the meaning of life, the purpose of our existence, is not really raised. These catechisms are compilations which bring together what the faithful must know about the creed, the Our Father, the ten commandments, the sacraments, Christian righteousness, and, in the case of Bellarmine, many other points, including even the rosary. The idea was not to delve into man's own questions but rather to explain and instruct, drawing on the catechist's knowledge as a source, and also in order to exhort people to live a Christian life. Such a catechism does not really lead to an exchange or dialogue; it rather 'talks at'.

THE MALINES FORMULA AND RELATED DOCUMENTS

Inspired by Canisius, Coster wrote a catechism in 1590 and 1604; he was followed by Makeblijde in 1609. This was the Malines catechism which would be very influential in Western Europe.

Here the question which concerns us is for the first time put quite explicitly in a Catholic text. I quote from the 1611 edition: 'For what end has man been created by God?—In order to know, love and serve God in this life and to enjoy and behold Him hereafter in eternal life'.[7]

Or in the French text (1672): 'For what end has God created us and put us into this world?—In order to know, love and serve Him and so to obtain life eternal'.[8]

This text seems to be the most common I could find, in spite of minor nuances, such as 'life eternal' occasionally becoming 'paradise' round about 1800, or 'heaven' about 1900.

Napoleon, one of the first to try to impose a unitary catechism, almost literally repoduces this text at the end of the *abrégé de l'Histoire Sainte*.[9]

This text is found in France till after the second World War, and in Canada, but just as easily in Africa, in Rwanda-Urundi or the Upper Volta.

In English-speaking countries children learn the same answer. Thus in the United States the *Catechism of Christian Doctrine* (Baltimore, 1885) says: 'Why did God make you?—God made me to know Him, to love Him, and to serve Him in this world, and to be happy with Him for ever in the next'.[10] We find practically the same text in England, Ireland or the Philippines, right into the fifties of this century.

But in 1941 a revised edition appeared in the United States which gives the answer as: 'God made me to show forth His goodness and to share with us His everlasting happiness in heaven'.[11] It is not clear whether the first half of this sentence refers to life on this earth, but it looks like that in all probability.

In Germany, too, this text is the most common. Deharbe took it over in his catechism (1850), which spread over the German-speaking countries and Poland. It says: 'Why have you been created?—I have been created in order to know God, to love Him and to serve Him, and thus be saved'.[12]

Even the new German *Katholischer Katechismus* of 1955 still says more or less the same, and this text passed to many countries: 'Why are we on this earth?—We are on this earth to know God, to love Him, to serve Him and one day to live with Him for all eternity'.[13]

In 1912 Pius X tried again to launch a universal catechism, which only succeeded in most Latin countries. It once again repeats the text of 'our' question in the same way: 'For what end has God created us?—God has created us to know Him, to love Him and to serve Him in this life, and to enjoy Him in the other life, in paradise'.[14]

Cardinal P. Gasparri, too, made once again an attempt at a universal catechism—which was nowhere taken up—and used the same text.[15]

And much earlier, in 1839, even the Greek Orthodox Church had incorporated this text in its 'small catechism' at the Synod of St Petersburg.[16] Towards the middle of the nineteenth century we occasionally come across a shorter, and in my opinion poorer, formula in the editions of the Malines catechism. So, for instance, in 1842: 'For what end has man been created?—In order to serve God in this life and to behold Him for all eternity hereafter'.[17] But what follows in this text is interesting: 'Has man not been created to enjoy himself in this life and to gather riches?—No; but to serve God.—Is man then not allowed to enjoy himself and to take care of his temporal affairs?—Yes, indeed, but he must direct all this towards the service of God . . .'[18] This shorter edition appears also (but without the addition) in Linden, who revised Deharbe in 1900, and this edition was taken over in some German dioceses and in the Netherlands.[19] It is, however, curious that the same shorter version had already appeared in the Anglican *Westminster Catechism*, the shorter catechism of 1647: 'What is the chief end of man?—Man's chief end is to glorify God and to enjoy Him for ever'.[20] Or in the *Catechismus Major:* 'What is man's highest and most important end?—Man's highest and most important end is to glorify God and to enjoy Him perfectly for all eternity'.[21] Is this then the origin of this text? I have not been able to trace it any further.

The Free Churches, too, spoke with the same voice: in 1823 the Methodists drew up a confession of faith which said in its chapter 'Of regeneration': 'This change is wrought in order that men may glorify God by bringing forth the fruits of righteousness, and purifying the soul, so as to be meet to enjoy fellowship with God for ever'.[22]

It seems to me that we find a much richer view in Hirscher, the bible-inspired pastoral theologian who, however, was not recognized in his own day. In his draft for a catechism (1842) we read: 'If, then, God has created man in the way you have said, what was the end for which He destined him?—This is clearly shown by the gifts and qualities which He has bestowed on him. Man must become and be that for which he has received the ability from God. Therefore he must know God, love God, obey God, do the works of God, and in heart and deed be holy, like God: he must do all this more and more. And he must recognize himself and the world around him, love himself and his fellow men, be good to himself and them, and fulfil his post on earth as God's representative, and in honour of God. All this more and more. And when at last he has been proved true and found perfect he will be transferred from the state of training and testing to the state of those that are true and perfect, i.e. the state of ineffable bliss in heaven. Expressed in few words we therefore say: God has created man in order to know Him, to love Him and to be blessed eternally.—But if man has been so highly placed through God's grace, what follows from that?—That this implies a terrible responsibility and an incredible hostility towards himself if man does not develop the gifts he has received from God and does not use them for the honour of God and for his own welfare and that of mankind'.[23]

Going back to the other formulas we find that all the questions, whether followed by the long or the short answer, fall into two categories: Why are we on this earth? or: Why has God created us? It is also interesting that some catechisms begin with this question while in others it appears much later (e.g., in France it occurs as question 63) after a more or less ample discussion of God, the Trinity, creation in general, and the angels. In such cases the question occurs usually somewhere in the instruction about man and the fall. One might be tempted to read those catechisms which begin with the question, especially when formulated as 'Why are we on this earth?', as intended to start from the human angle, but a closer look rules this out. The questions are rather meant to be a method to facilitate the answers. Real existential questioning was apparently not the main consideration.

NEW APPROACHES TO THE OLD QUESTION

In the long list of questions and answers one is struck by the Dutch catechism of 1948: 'Why are we on this earth?—We are on this earth in order to serve God and thus to be happy here and hereafter'.[24] This was the first time that I had noticed such a positive mention of happiness on this earth, and the idea is clearly to indicate that a good life brings with it also human happiness. It sounds positive, but this is all and it is not further pursued. Moreover, all the negative experiences of misery and guilt which make the question about the meaning of life so difficult to understand seem to be completely ignored.

The first catechism which makes the attempt to take this question seriously in all its complexity seems to be the *New Catechism. Catholic Faith for Adults*. It appeared in the Netherlands in 1966 and the English version in 1967. Part One is entitled: 'The Mystery of Existence'. The centre here is man, searching for an answer with all his grandeur and misery within a growing world. It mentions the longing for happiness in the narrow and the broad sense, the desire to be good, the straining after the infinite good, but also our vulnerability through sickness, disappointment, guilt and death. Then this catechism talks about the good news, brought by Jesus Christ, which does not remove the mystery but *does* point the way towards an answer. The whole book—no longer an interplay of short and clear questions and answers but a constant struggle for deeper understanding, for over 500 pages—constantly returns to this questioning, not so much in order to provide answers as to grope for an answer under the guidance of Jesus and his Church.[25]

It seems that since then several attempts have been made to talk about the Christian faith in this or some better way from the angle of man's search for the meaning of his existence. Thus, in 1976, *The teaching of Christ. A Catholic catechism for adults* (not an official catechism) started with this kind of question in 'the hope of our calling', but it is barely pursued in the rest of the book.[26] On the other hand, the *Evangelischer Erwachsenekatechismus. Kursbuch des Glaubens*, collectively commissioned by the Evangelical-Lutheran Church of Germany in 1975, is truly fascinating.[27] It is impossible to show in the present brief space how the approach from man's questioning has been dealt with here. Perhaps the following quotation may give some indication of what the authors meant to do:

> Whoever wants to present the content of the Christian faith, can do so in various ways. He can put together what the Bible has reported; he can relate the origins of the faith and how people of many generations experienced it; he can explain how everything follows from one basic tenet. But he can also start from the questions put by his contemporaries and present the Christian faith as an answer to these questions. This is the approach mainly followed in this book. In many sections it tries to throw some light on the human situation, to spell out questions that arise from it, and, together with the reader, to look for answers in the Christian message. This is not an easy approach because the Christian faith has no solution for every single problem. Apart from this there are not only questions which come over loud and clear but also other ones, which nobody expresses publicly but are no less in need of an answer. They cannot be ignored. Nor can the Christian faith be limited to what it offers us to cope with the questions of the day. It does not just provide some answers, but also brings out new questions and, last not least, makes us listen to questions which God puts to man (p. 36).

It speaks about God as 'on his way to man'; about man as 'himself on the way'; about Jesus as 'the way and the life'; about 'life in the world' (private life, life in one's occupation and life in society) and only after that about 'life with the Church'.[28]

What I have given here is but an outline. But, then, the idea was simply to provide a backcloth against which the ideas contained in the other articles might stand out more clearly: what were the answers we have been given up till the present? To what extend do we need a new kind of answer?—Or, indeed, a new kind of question?

Notes

1. *Die Bekenntnisschriften der evangelisch-lutherischen Kirche* ²(Göttingen, 1952).

2. Wilhelm Niesel, *Bekenntnisschriften und Kirchenordnungen der nach Gottes Wort reformierten Kirche*² (Zollikon-Zürich, 1938).

3. Ibid.

4. Ibid.

5. E. F. Karl Müller, *Die Bekenntnisschriften der reformierten Kirche* (Leipzig, 1903).

6. *Catechismus Romanus* (ed. Antverpia, 1596).

7. *Catechismus, dat is, de christelijke Leeringe* (Antwerp, 1611).

8. *Catéchisme ou Instructions chrétiennes pour le diocèse de Liège* (Maastricht, 1672).

9. *Catéchisme à l'usage de toutes les églises de l'empire français* (Paris, 1806).

10. *A Catechism of Christian Doctrine* (publ. by ecclesiastical authority, n.d.).

11. Ibid. (Paterson, N.Y., 1941).

12. *Katholischer Katechismus oder Lehrbegriff* (Regensburg, 1850).

13. *Katholischer Katechismus der Bistümer Deutschlands* (Freiburg, 1955).

14. *Primi Elementi della Dottrina Cristiana* (Turin, n.d.).

15. Petrus Card. Gasparri, *Catechismus Catholicus* (Typis Polygl. Vat., 1930).

16. D. Karl Buchrucker, *Die Normalkatechismen der christlichen Kirchen* (Nürnberg, 1890).

17. *Mechelschen Catechismus met uytleggingen op iedere vraag* (Malines, 1842).

18. Ibid.

19. Jakob Linden, S. J., *Der mittlere Deharbe'sche Katechismus* (Regensburg, Rome, New York, 1900).

20. E. F. Karl Müller (see note 5).

21. Ibid.

22. Ibid.

23. Dr. Johann-Baptist Hirscher, *Katechismus der christ-katholischen Religion* (Karlsruhe and Freiburg, 1842).

24. *Katechismus of Christelijke Leer ten gebruike der Nederlandse bisdommen* (Roermond, 1948).

25. *De Nieuwe Katechismus. Geloofsverkondiging voor volwassenen* (Hilversum, 's-Hertogenbosch, Roermond-Maaseik, 1966).

26. R. Lawler, OFM Cap., a. o., *The teaching of Christ. A catholic catechism for Adults* (Huntington, Ind., 1976).

27. W. Jentsch a.o., *Evangelischer Erwachsenenkatechismus. Kursbuch des Glaubens* (Gütersloh, 1975).

28. Ibid.

Max Charlesworth

Anthropological Presuppositions of the Question 'Has Life a Meaning?'

WHAT philosophical presuppositions about the nature of man and his situation in the world have to be made if the first question of the catechism is to be meaningful? We know that for many people today the question, 'Why did God make me?' (or, in its secular form, 'What is the meaning of life?') does not any longer have a clear and urgent meaning. It is not that such people are stupid and of bad faith, or that they are flippant and unthinking hedonists living only for the present moment. Rather, for such people questions about the meaning of human existence do not make sense any more since, so they claim, the conditions under which such questions make sense or have meaning no longer obtain. Such questions, it is argued, can only arise within a certain cultural context or 'thought-structure' or (to use Michel Foucault's convenient term) *epistème*, and such a context or structure is no longer viable. In a culture shaped on the one hand by scientific naturalism, which abstracts from questions of value and meaning, and on the other hand by the various forms of 'idealism' or 'constructivism' which see value and meaning as human constructs imported by man into existence, the first question of the catechism seems naive and pointless.

EMPIRISM

If human existence is seen as being part of the natural order, and if the natural order is seen within an empiricist perspective according to which nature is simply the sum total of the 'brute facts' (the 'value-free' facts) of physics and chemistry, then human life itself comes to be seen as a 'brute' and 'value-free' fact. Within the context of scientific empiricism we cannot ask whether the world has a purpose or a meaning or whether it is good or bad, and equally we cannot ask whether human life has a meaning and value. Like the brute facts of physics human life simply *is*. In the same way, if value and meaning are human constructs imposed by man upon reality and upon human existence, then it is simple-minded to ask, 'Why did God make me?' or 'What is the meaning of life?'. It is I who must make myself to be, I who must endow my life with a meaning, for life does not have any ready-made meaning. Nietzsche has expressed this point perfectly in *The Genealogy of Morals:*[1]

> To view nature as if it were a proof of the goodness and providence of a God; to interpret history to the glory of a divine reason, as the perpetual witness to a moral world order and moral intentions; to interpret one's own experiences, as pious men long interpreted them, as if everything were preordained, everything a sign, everything sent for the salvation of the soul—that now belongs to the *past*, that has the conscience *against* it, that seems to every more sensitive conscience indecent, dishonest, mendacious, feminism, weakness, cowardice . . .

If we look a little more carefully at the two great thought-structures or *epistèmes* just mentioned[2] within which, as we have said, the first question of the catechism becomes meaningless, then we may perhaps be able, in an indirect way, to discern the anthropological presuppositions required for that question to be *meaningful* to contemporary man.

I cannot here study in any detail the various historical forces that brought about the emergence of the natural sciences in the sixteenth and seventeenth centuries and that caused those sciences to be allied with an empiricist epistemology and a naturalistic world-view. There is nothing in the intrinsic logic of the natural sciences that makes such an alliance with empiricism or naturalism either necessary or inevitable. Nevertheless, the scientific view of the world and of man, which has had such a powerful influence on the modern mind, has been for the most part radically empiricist and radically naturalistic.

Within the context of Humean empiricism the world is simply the totality of facts—facts which are simply *there* in spatio-temporal juxtaposition. It is a world in which the categories of possibility and necessity do not operate and a world in which there are no causal connections between the 'loose and separate' atomic facts. It is also a world devoid of values. In themselves the empirical facts are neither good nor bad, neither valuable nor valueless.

NATURALISM

Within the context of naturalism man is seen as part of nature, nature in turn being defined as that which is the object of classical physics and chemistry. Since, once again, the world of physics and chemistry is 'value-free', values can only enter into this world through man. Values are born, so to speak, from the meeting of human needs and interests with the world of neutral physico-chemical facts. However, since man himself is part of nature his needs and interests and attitudes are themselves explicable in naturalistic, physico-chemical, terms, so that ultimately, as in the work of B. F. Skinner,[3] values simply denote the way in which the human organism—with its biological 'givens'—interacts with and adapts itself to its environment in order to survive. In the Skinnerian world the question, 'What is the meaning of life?' is translated into, 'How can that part of nature which we call the human organism interact with and adapt itself to other parts of nature in order to secure its survival?'.

It is not my purpose here to chart the history of this movement of thought and to show the alliances and 'marriages of convenience' it has entered into with other ideas and movements. (One could, for instance, mention the fortuitous conjunction between scientific empiricism and naturalism and the movement of liberalism—science being seen as the agency of liberation from religious superstition and mythical ways of thinking, and the scientific spirit—supposedly experimental, non-dogmatic and methodologically tolerant—being directly linked with the moral and political values of liberalism.[4]) It is enough to say that within the devalued world of naturalism man simply *is*; he exists with a given biological structure and given needs and interests; he interacts with his environment, and he survives. No doubt it is possible to formulate a kind of humanism within this framework—as Freud, Huxley, Monod and others have tried to do—but it is a humanism of a radically attenuated and impoverished kind and one with, so to speak, an extremely limited vocabulary. However, even if it is possible to give some kind of meaning to life within this context, it is clearly not possible for the kind of meaning and value that has any relevance for the Christian to exist in this climate. Science and the values implicit in science (the recognition of the autonomy and the 'sacredness' of nature and of man's solidarity with nature) certainly do have relevance for

Christianity, but science interpreted through the lenses of empiricism and naturalism produces a world where it is no longer possible for the great Christian questions to be asked.

CONSTRUCTIVISM

Within the perspectives of what we have called 'constructivism', values and meaning are seen as constructs which we impose upon reality and human existence. In its purely epistemological form constructivism is of course classically expressed in Kant's *The Critique of Pure Reason*, and in its moral and social form in the complex movement of Promethean humanism which runs from Hegel, through Feuerbach and Marx and Nietzsche to Sartre. For Marx the world we know and live in is the world we ourselves have made—the world that is the product of *praxis*—and we know ourselves and 'make' ourselves in the process of our interchanges with the world. The world has no intrinsic meaning apart from human *praxis*, and equally man's existence has no ready-made or given meaning apart from his creative transformations of nature. As Marx puts it: 'The practical construction of an objective world, the manipulation of inorganic nature, is the conformation of man as a conscious species-being. . . . He no longer reproduces himself merely intellectually, as in consciousness, but actually and in a real sense, and he sees his own reflection in a world which he has constructed'.[5]

From a rather different point of view, for Nietzsche meaning and value are human constructs. With the death of God man must become his own God: that is to say, his own creator and lawgiver. For Nietzsche the full implications of what this means becomes clear only when we have confronted the possibility of nihilism. So he writes in *The Will to Power:* 'Scepticism regarding morality is what is decisive. The end of the moral interpretation of the world, which no longer has any sanction after it has tried to escape into some beyond, leads to nihilism. "All lacks meaning"'.[6] For Nietzsche there is a radical choice between belief in God on the one hand, and the acceptance and affirmation of human freedom and autonomy on the other. If there is a God then man cannot be fully free and autonomous; if we take man's freedom and autonomy *seriously* then there cannot be a God. No doubt Christianity has given value and meaning of a certain kind to human existence but it is a false kind of meaning which is incompatible with man's dignity and seriousness.

Sartre, in his pre-Marxist phase, expressed the same Nietzschean idea in his popular essay, *Existentialism and Humanism:*

The existentialist is strongly opposed to a certain type of secular moralism which seeks to suppress God at the least possible expense . . . In other words—and this is, I believe, the purport of all that we in France call radicalism—nothing will be changed if God does not exist; we shall rediscover the same norms of honesty, progress and humanity, and we shall have disposed of God as an out-of-date hypothesis which will die away quietly of itself. The existentialist, on the contrary, finds it extremely embarrasing that God does not exist, for there disappears with Him all possibility of finding values in an intelligible heaven. There can no longer be any good *a priori* since there is no infinite and perfect consciousness to think it. It is nowhere written that 'the good' exists, that one must be honest or must not lie, since we are now upon the plane where there are only men.[7]

Another version of constructivism is to be found in the contemporary semilogical and structualist movement. For de Saussure, the founding father of semiology, language is wholly a human creation: sounds and other physical objects have no signifying power in themselves but are endowed with the status of signs by man. This model of language has been adopted by structuralists such as Lévi-Strauss and Foucault and applied to the whole of man's social existence. However for the semiologists and structuralists it is not the individual who creates systems of meaning but society. Just as the individual speaker of a language operates within a linguistic system which is already constituted (though it can be enlarged and modified) so also, the individual finds himself in a social system—a tissue of social meanings and values—that is already determined for him. The semiologists also make the more radical point that, just as words have meaning and exist as signs wholly by virtue of their relationships (of opposition and difference) with other words ('in the linguistic system there are only differences with no positive terms'), so also in social existence it is differential relationships which are of primary importance. For de Saussure we must abandon the idea that words or linguistic phenomena have any 'substance' apart from the differential relationships which constitute them,[8] and in the same way the structuralists argue that we must get away from the idea of the individual existing apart from the network of differential social relationships. From this point of view the individual member of society only has meaning as a kind of nodal point of a tissue of relationships. This has led some of the structuralist thinkers to anti-humanistic conclusions. Thus Michel Foucault has spoken of the 'death of man', meaning by this that the whole conception of man found in classical humanism is now past. The subject or self is a construct, the product of a system of social conventions; in other words, the constructor is itself constructed.[9] Although for the semiologists meaning is a human creation—meaning comes into the world through man—this does not have the 'Promethean' and humanistic implications that it has for Marx or Nietzsche or Sartre.

So far we have seen in what contexts the first question of the catechism does *not* make sense. Within the 'value-free' world of scientific naturalism it is no longer possible to ask, 'Why did God make me?' or 'What is the meaning of life?'. And in the same way within the context of constructivism—represented variously by Kantianism, Promethean humanism and semiology—since man is the creator of meaning we cannot ask whether man himself has a meaning. Nevertheless, as we have seen, both the movement of scientific naturalism and the movement of Promethean humanism themselves enshrine certain undeniable values—a recognition of the 'sacredness' of nature and of man's solidarity with nature (powerfully emphasized by Teilhard de Chardin) in the one case, and a recognition of human freedom and creativity and autonomy in the other.

THE MEANING OF THE QUESTION

What then are the conditions of possiblity of meaning for the first question of the catechism in a world shaped by scientific naturalism and the various forms of constructivism? It would be simplistic to say that all we need do is to reject as false both these movements and to restore by *fiat* a sense of God as the author of existence and value and a sense of man's total dependence upon God. The question is *what* conception of God and of man's relationship to God is now possible? We cannot pretend that the scientific revolution has not happened and that the values represented in that revolution are not real. Equally we cannot pretend that Marx and Nietzsche have not occurred and that the question they put to Christianity—'How can one take human freedom and creativity and autonomy *seriously* and still believe that man was made by God?'—is not a real one. If the first question of the catechism only makes sense on the basis of philosophical presuppositions about the nature of man and his situation in the world that represents a return (*i*) to a naive pre-scientific world view, and (*ii*) to an unserious view of human freedom, then Christianity no longer has anything to say to contemporary men. To put the matter more positively, the first question of the catechism will only make sense to contemporary men if it is phrased in such a way that it takes account of what we have called the sacredness and autonomy of nature—seeing nature as having a value of its own and not just as a backdrop to the human drama—and on the other hand if it rethinks the ancient Christian definition of man as *imago Dei* and as co-creator with God.

Notes

1. F. Nietzsche, *The Genealogy of Morals,* third essay, section 27; trans. W. Kaufmann and R. J. Hollingdale (New York, 1969).

2. In fact, they are aspects of the same one structure and they exist in dialectical relationship with each other, very much in the way in which, in the epistemological sphere, Humean empiricism and Kantian idealism depend dialectically upon each other. Empiricism can only maintain its plausibility by its opposition to idealism and, *vice versa*, Kantianism derives its own appearance of plausibility from its opposition to Humean empiricism. In the same way naturalism and constructivism are parasitic upon each other.

3. B. F. Skinner, *Beyond Freedom and Dignity* (New York, 1971).

4. This alliance is expressed very clearly, for example, in the thought of nineteenth-century English liberal thinkers such as John Stuart Mill.

5. Karl Marx, *Economic and Philosophical Manuscripts* trans. T. B. Bottomore (London, 1963), 1st Ms, p. xxiv.

6. F. Nietzsche, *The Will to Power*, trans. W. Kaufmann (New York, 1967), Book 1, section iii.

7. Jean-Paul Sartre, *Existentialism and Humanism*, trans. P. Mairet (London, 1961), p. 10.

8. F. de Saussure, *Cours de linguistique générale* (Paris, 1963), pp. 168–9.

9. M. Foucault, *Les Mots et les choses* (Paris, 1966). J. Derrida, *De la grammatologie* (Paris 1967).

Jacques Pohier

Why are We on This Earth? A Comment Based on Psychoanalytic Concepts

THE general theme of this issue was discussed for the first time at the *Concilium* meeting in Munich in May 1975. I asked Hans Küng on that occasion whether the ecumenical context of the problems involved would include not only the various Christian denominations but all those who, when faced with the question 'Why are we here?' offer as their main (and sometimes sole) answer: 'Because one day a man and a woman—our father and mother—made love and a child—me—was the result'. He told me that my worry depended on the French formulation of the question in which the word 'why', 'pourquoi', can refer either to the effective cause or to the final cause, but that in German this ambiguity was impossible since there the word used for 'why' in this instance is 'wozu', and 'wozu' refers only to the ultimate cause, wheras the effective causality I was speaking of supposed the use of another why-word, namely 'warum'. Philology put my question out of court in the German-speaking context, which in English might be represented as *why* ('warum') and *wherefore* ('wozu').

But it wasn't quite out of court, since later on Hans Küng had occasion to ask me for some comments on the topic from the viewpoint of psychoanalysis. But when I mulled over the question from my childhood catechism, 'Why are we on earth?', all the ideas arising from psychoanalytic considerations very much depended on both the questions 'why?'—namely, on 'warum' and 'wozu', why and wherefore, and hence on the combined questions of effective and ultimate cause. When I hear the question raised of my ideal: what is the purpose of your life, what meaning is their in your life?, the psychoanalyst in me

25

forces me to ask about the ideal of those who conceived me. To what end did they conceive me? What path and what meaning did their desire trace out for my life? What desire in them made me? In short, in order to have some idea of what is in front of me and towards what I should(?) go, I have to know what was at my origin (in other words, behind me), and therefore passes through me only to be projected before me as my ideal. My finality is my finality—my meaning—only because it was the finality and the meaning which those who conceived me allocated to themselves in that act of my conception. That is the 'why I was conceived' that answers the 'why, or to what end, was I conceived?'

This conversion of the ultimate into the effective 'why' should not astonish those who ask themselves the question of why they are here in the context of the catechism or of a confession of faith. In fact, I answer this question by telling myself what purpose God has in creating me and in redeeming me. Whoever asks about his destiny and what road his life should take if it is to be meaningful is required to look at the divine aspect of things. It is that aspect and the way in which God sees man which enable him to find both his destiny and his way to that end. It is God's will in regard to my life which defines my end in life. Or, to put it in terms which are often thought to be over-anthropomorphic, but why should talk of God's desire be more anthropomorphic than talk of his will or intention or plan?), it is the desire of God in creating and redeeming me which defines the end and the meaning of my existence.

An essential objective of Christian life is to interiorize that will, intention and desire: and to make them my own will, intention and desire. I shall truly have reached my goal and meaning when I coincide with the goal and meaning ordained by my God in creating and redeeming me. That is why the theme of *redditus ad Deum* is so strong in Christian spirituality. Of course this topic sometimes indicates a more or less regressive return to the origins, a more or less mythical reconstitution of a previous state of fusion with a God who seems rather like a maternal bosom in which it would be ultimate bliss to lose oneself. But even when the topic indicates a construction, a future which it is up to God and man to make (even when it is a question more of a future to discover than a past to restore), the Christian journey seems like a return to our source.

Moreover, when it speaks of a Christian death and of reaching a new and definitive life, Christan piety often says: 'It has pleased God to restore to himself our brother X . . .' or 'X has returned to the Father' or 'to his Father's mansion'.

Psychoanalysis is concerned with a more human form of fatherhood and motherhood. That changes both a few and a lot of things in the way in which our ideal, and the aim and meaning of our life, are determined by the aim and the desire of those who conceived us when they did so. The essence of what is changed by this probably depends on what I call the contingency of our conception. This contingency does not modulate the way in which God brings about and intends our origin, but affects the way in which our father and mother bring about and intend our origin, which is true also of any other person or occasion contributing to that conception (in the broad sense) of what we are and what we should be in order truly to be ourselves. That contingency in regard to them becomes necessity in regard to us. Origin in this case is much more contingent than the way in which God is origin. But it is an origin which is certainly much more a matter of necessity than the way in which God is origin.

WHO WAS DESIRED?

Of course we might well not have been desired at all. Our parents did not want children, say, or found they had enough already, or didn't happen to want any at that point in their lives. During the discussions on the new legislation regarding abortion in France (from 1972 to 1975), the question asked by many adolescents (at an age when it is true, of course, that there is a special need to be reassured about one's identity) was: Did my mother want to have an abortion when she was pregnant with me? It is possible that we were not desired as we are; they wanted a boy, and a girl happened along. And there are those who will probably never live in the body proper to their own sex because that sex will always be opposed to the desire of those who conceived them. There are many fates determined irretrievably because one was the child which replaced the older sister or brother who died young, or because one's dead brother or sister couldn't be forgotten, or because one couldn't replace the brother whom our mother lost when he was young or the sister our father lost once. There is another child who is more difficult to replace and whose weight can even more heavily burden our fates: it is the child which our father or mother did not become.— Perhaps because in the infinity of generations their own parents had decided they ought to be not the child they were but another: that other child they hated having to be while being forced to want to be it.

The fact that our parents might not have wanted us, or that they could have wanted a different child, often decides our fate by assigning us a role other than the role we can follow, yet one that we have to play in order to coincide with the desire that conceived and shaped us. But what is hardly reassuring for our identitity is also very injurious as far as our narcissism is concerned. For it it tantamount to saying that we are not the centre of gravity of the relationship which unites our parents. We are only a result, even an accident, of that relationship. The megalomania of our imperious longing is almost intolerably rejected by the inescapable fact that, even if the desire for a child is undoubtedly fundamentally present in every sex act, our parents were not thinking of us when they made love, and they did not make love because of us but because of themselves—the two 'whys'. In view of the assurance of so many centuries of Christian doctrine and practice about procreation as the first end of marrage, I have often thought that it was not an instance only of a great repression of pleasure or of a social control of sexuality, but also a question of our narcissism protesting, and thus re-establishing our primacy over our parents and trying to make us the centre of gravity of their relationship and their pleasure. Conrad Stein, a French psychoanalyst, indicates appropriately the position which this intention has in the psychic make-up: 'I invent this scence of my birth; I am my own inventor; in making myself that which ordains my parents' meeting I conceive myself. All that I did can result only in me, hence my hesitation in acknowledging that my parents' meeting could have taken place outside me, before me, that it was an historical event'.[1] The fact that the affirmation of the primacy of procreation among the ends of sexual life should serve the exaltation of the child's narcissism enables us to understand how that affirmation occupies such a position in a religion which has so exalted the Son's position that it seemed to Freud (as it does to many Jews and Muslims) that he had obscured the Father's superiority.

A CHILD TO BE KILLED

Heredity, which is conveyed through chromosomes, is insignificant in comparison with the desire our parents had for us. That desire was all the more effective in that they were often and largely unware of it; and in that it concerned us from before our conception, and throughout our childhood, youth and even our life thereafter. Until we die, however old we are then, we are inhabited by a child who is the child our parents' desire made us be; whom the phantasies and desires of those who conceived us project through us and before us, as that which we ought to be: the why and wherefore with which they dialogue through us and which make us the stage where they encounter their own desires and their own phantasies. We are both enclosed and framed in their fantasy child, and lifted out of ourselves and ahead of ourselves towards that child which we have to be in order to be ourselves.

That is why the French psychoanalyst Serge Leclaire wrote: 'Psychoanalytic practice depends on the demonstration of the constant operation of a death force; and that force consists in killing the miraculous (or terrifying) child which, from generation to generation, testifies to the dreams and desires of its parents; there is life only at the price of the assassination of the first alien image in which each person is born . . . The unconscious representation of the mother's phantasy (i.e., of the phantasy the mother has about her child) . . . is unconsciously designated by the subject as the most intimate, alien and disturbing of all. It is seen as a representative that never was and never will be, and that on the other hand by its absolutely alien nature will constitute the most secret and most sacred aspect of what . . . it is. It is this privileged unconscious representative that I call the "primary narcisstic representative". The child to kill, the child to glorify, the all-powerful child, the terrifying child; that is the figure of the primary narcissistic representative. Cursed, a universal inheritance and the object of an neccesary yet impossible assassination'.[2]

Why are we on this earth? For the reason why our parents made us? We don't really know, except that we probably aren't the reason. We know that they wanted us to be, but what an alien and tedious knowledge that is: the knowledge of the mark in us of their desire. We know what we have to be in order to be: that each day we must experience 'that death of the miraculous or terrifying child that we were in the dreams of those who made us or saw us born'.[3]

THE IMAGINARY CHILD

The paradox is that the psychoanalytical effort and even the work of existence is both the assassination of a child, and the making of a child. 'The reconstruction of the child that the patient was is one of the essential aspects of analysis'.[4] But this does not imply, as a too genetic notion of psychoanalysis would have it, a self-discovery by means of a detailed pursuit of the historical process by which the patient passes from his babyhood to the present moment. It is even less a matter of what Paul Ricoeur wrongly suggests in his interpretation of psychoanalysis;[5] of an exploration which is intended to show the subject his archaeology and then shut him up in it. It is very much a question of a construction which ordains the present and opens up the future. The experience of cure shows that the patient wanted both (whatever his sex) the psychoanalyst (whatever his sex) to give him a child, and to be the psychoanalyst's child; and hence to be both mother and child simultaneously; to be, that is, at one and the same time his own mother and the child of his mother. Every human being, in my opinion, bears within him as one of his most fundamental phantasies, the desire to be the person who gives his mother a child; to be the mother who was given the child that one is; and to be the child that his mother wanted him to be.

Conrad Stein organized an extremely profound and original presentation of the psychoanalytical cure and the constitution of the subject around this theme of the 'imaginary child', which results from all those child-images that the patient wants to be and to produce: a kind of umbilicus of what he is and of what he will have to be: 'To construct the history of the child one has been, who is at the same time self and product of self, is less a matter of producing one of the avatars of the imaginary child, than of enclosing it in a work whose form is never definitive, never finished'.[6] We might well apply to the existence of the human subject what Stein said of the process of analysis: 'Its end—its why—is to bring about the recognition by a third party of a work which is none other than its creator's own person. Such a work is an imaginary work in the sense that it can take shape only in its avatars: a child represented in thought by the child that one was, as also by the child that one would like to have; it is an imaginary child'.[7]

Why are we on earth? The wherefore which could make life meaningful is both the constitution of self as one's own work, and the necessity bringing about an acknowledgment both of the author and of the result of that work; of, that is, self as subject. The task is just as vital (because abstention from it is fatal), and just as impossible, both to accomplish and to revive, as that which consists (according to Serge Leclaire) in reliving each day the death of the miraculous child which we were in the dreams of those who made us.

THE IDEAL OF THE EGO

The question of the relation between our two whys—our why and our wherefore—can be approached from another viewpoint which is easily accessible for those who know the works of Freud and the notion of the personality derived from them in the psychological and educational sciences. Since 1914, since, that is, a period before the development of the second theme (ego—id—super-ego) and therefore before mentioning the super-ego, Freud introduced the term 'ego-ideal'[8] by which he means 'an instance of the personality resulting from the convergence of narcissism (idealization of self) and identifications with one's parents, their substitutes and collective ideals'.[9] Freud notes: 'What a man projects before himself as his ideal is the substitute for the lost narcissism of his childhood; of that time when he was his own ideal for himself'.[10] Hence the ideal, what lies ahead, the wherefore, is a projection ahead of self of what is behind self. When he introduces and develops the super-ego theory, Freud tends to use the super-ego and the ego-ideal almost as synonyms, to designate that which unites the functions of taboo and ideal.

This super-ego is formed by identification with one's parents in correlation with the decline of the Oedipus complex. There the subject is constituted by interiorization of the parental ideal and parental taboos. Yet we must follow Freud in stating that 'the child's super-ego is not formed in his parents' image, but in the image of their super-ego. It assumes the same content and becomes the representative of tradition, of all those value-judgments which thus continue for generations'. This constitution of the subject by identification with parental values is the paradigm for further identification of those values, of moral, social or institutional instances or 'personalities'.

Hence the ideal the subject has of himself, the goal he assigns to life and to himself, the meaning in terms of which he decides his future orientation and judges his present or his past, comes to him from all those who conceived him and from the way in which they did it. That does not mean of course that it is impossible to discover future or autonomy in the present. Paul Ricoeur was certainly wrong to emphasize the opposition between archaeology and teleology in order to claim that psychoanalysis was no more than and reduced everything to the former, and closed and was closed to the latter.[11] But that means that we cannot be the children of our works unless we are the children of the works of all those who conceived us. That does not however exclude the fact that in order to live we have to kill the child that we were in their dreams.

WHY AND WHEREFORE ARE NOT NAMES OF GOD

Are we in the same situation in regard to the intention, plan and desire we accord to God regarding the goal and meaning of our existence? God's desire is both less contingent and less a matter of necessity than that of our parents and of all those whose desire helped to make us. It is less contingent since it has less to do with the vicissitudes of a history as unusual as that of our father, our mother or any other family figure. And it is not so much a matter of necessity, since—if the term is permissible—God can venture something more easily than human procreators, than beings whom he created in his image by giving them intelligence and freedom, and who exist autonomously and decide their fate only so far as they can. While it is the most necessary, in the metaphysical sense, of all those causalities which can affect us, the divine causality should seem the least contingent and the most liberating. There is no reason to kill the child we were in God's dream.

But that only goes to show that the narcissism of the human being can hardly accept such a notion of God's desire in relation to him, since he must henceforth cease to see himself as the child of which God dreamed. We must not forget, in fact, that it is partly the narcissism of the subject which draws this miraculous and terrifying child as he was in his parents' dream. Of course the phantasies his parents had of him made him like that. But it is also a phantasmal necessity for the subject to present himself thus and to tell himself that his parents shaped him thus; for it is that which allows the subject to present himself as the centre of the parental universe, the centre of the desires and phantasms of his parents. I have already said that the child is the centre and goal of his parents' sexual activity. It is no less necessary to see oneself as the centre and goal of God's creative and redemptive action.

Of course we can't really put it like that. But we can say the equivalent in making each contingent element of our life, however small it may be, the result and the goal of God's explicit and formal desire. We can see the least detail of our existence as desired by God: Why am I a man rather than a woman? Why am I French rather than German or Chinese? Why do I live in the twentieth rather than the thirteenth or thirty-fifth century? Why have I met this woman rather than another—this friend—this enemy—this master—this disciple? Every time I answer: because God wanted it that way. Therefore I can see every detail of my own life as the trace and result of a desire of God's. Therefore we have a 'why' which grounds a 'wherefore', since it enables me to see as meaningful the most fortuitous and contingent elements of my life, which thus take on a finality, a 'wherefore', and not the least of all wherefores, since in God there is a wherefore which takes their existence into account.

The framework of this article does not allow me to offer a critique of such an idea of God, of his providence and his causality, nor of the idea of man behind such an idea of God.[12] But in order to formulate very briefly the result for me (as believer) of the experience of psychoanalysis and of contact with its theory and practice, I should say at least that I can no longer see God's desire in regard to man and the world as explaining why and as giving a wherefore-explanation of the world as a whole and of the human condition and the very least detail of world and condition. Nor can I see God's desire in regard to me as explaining and giving a meaning to all my own life and to its least detail. In a sense it is true that I have no answer to the question 'Why am I here?' other than this: 'Because my father, Etienne Pohier, and my mother, Eugénie Boulanger, made me—as they made my sister and my two brothers—on one of the occasions when they made love'. And that, after all, is not so bad a way to come to, or so bad a reason to be brought into, existence.

But God does not seem to me to offer a reply either to the why-question or to the wherefore-question; either in regard to my life, or in regard to man, or in regard to the world. God does not offer me an explanation nor the finality of that which is. God is an event, a being who breaks into my life and who breaks into the world of men. The good news of the Gospel is not that we shall now have an answer to the why and wherefore of existence; it is that God can be with us and that we can be with him. And if I pose a why and wherefore in regard to this subject it is in terms as anthropomorphic as those of the Gospel and the Bible; it is the why and wherefore that one always asks about and for in love: why does he love me? How can he love me? Why is *he?* Why is he who he is? Why and wherefore is he him? Why and wherefore does he want to be who he is with me? I confess, in the sense of the confession of faith, that God does not allow me to answer any other why and wherefore than those. That does not mean of course that I will necessarily find answers elsewhere. But I am only a man. And God is my *God,* not my wherefore or my why.

Translated by John Griffiths

Notes

1. C. Stein, *L'Enfant imaginaire* (Paris, 1975), p. 315.
2. S. Leclaire, *On tue un enfant* (Paris, 1975), pp. 15 and 21–2.
3. Ibid., p. 13.
4. C. Stein, 'A qui revient la paternité de l'oeuvre dans la situation analytique, au patient ou au psychanalyste?', in *Interprétation* (Montreal) 3 (1969), no. 1–2, p. 98. Also in C. Stein, *La mort d'Oedipe* (Paris, 1977), p. 101.
5. Cf. P. Ricoeur, *De l'Interprétation: Essai sur Freud* (Paris, 1965).
6. C. Stein, 'A qui revient . . .', p. 111; *La mort . . .* , p. 116.
7. C. Stein, *L'Enfant imaginaire*, p. 372.
8. We must not confuse the 'ego-ideal' with which I am concerned here with another Freudian term: the 'ideal ego'. Theoreticians of psychoanalysis are concerned with the differences and relations between them. Cf. Laplance and Pontalis, *Vocabulaire de la Psychanalyse* (Paris, 1967), pp. 184–86 and 255–56. See too D. Laganche, 'La psychanalyse et la structure de la personnalité, *La Psychanalyse* 6 (1961), esp. pp. 36–47, and all the proceedings of the twenty-third congress of psychoanalysts from the Latin countries (Paris, 1973), which was wholly concerned with the ego-ideal. *Revue française de psychanalyse* 37 (1973), pp. 705–1200.
9. Laplanche and Pontalis, op. cit., p. 184.
10. S. Freud, *Collected Papers*, vol 4 (London, 1924–5).
11. Cf. P. Ricoeur, op. cit.
12. See J. Pohier, *Quand je dis Dieu* (Paris, 1977), in which I undertake this critique at length.

PART II

Is the Old Answer Still Adequate?

David Tracy

A Catholic Answer

AS PROFESSOR van de Poel's article makes clear the traditional, main-line Catholic answer to the question 'Why did God make me' is some version of the basic response 'To know, love and serve Him in this world and to be happy with Him forever in the world to come'. Indeed as his excellent historical survey makes clear not until the 'Dutch Catechism' (the *New Catechism*) is there a more positive mention of 'terrestrial happiness'. Since that time, the focus of the answer has shifted still more in terms of the changed question of the very meaning of our lives in time and in history.

THE CHANGING SITUATION OF THE QUESTION

One way to note the importance of this shift is to focus initially not on the answer but on the question. Indeed, as the intrinsic logic of all hermeneutical understanding clarifies, the basic task in interpreting any answer is to clarify first and foremost the question to which it responds.

In that context, the most familiar, post-Reformation Catholic catechetical response cited above expresses a question 'Why did God make me?' which seems well suited to its situation. By 'situation' here, let us note, one need not refer merely to the particular historical events and personages which occasioned the specific question. Rather, one may employ the term 'situation' in a more elusive but more radical sense. For example, Paul Tillich employs this suggestive expression to refer to basic *ethos*, major existential questions disclosed in the major cultural realities (art, philosophy, religion) of any given period. Some candidates for the major existential questions of any given period and of particular periods in Christian thought are: the question of morality and finitude for the Greek patristic writers; the question of order and harmony in a universe of both faith and reason for the medievals; the question of personal forgiveness for sins for Luther; the question of very meaning of an authentic existence in the midst of a cultural crisis of meaninglessness for Tillich himself and other 'existentialist' theologians; the question of responding with authenticity to the linked limit-situations of alienation in first-world societies and oppression and exploitation in third and fourth world societies for contemporary 'liberation' and 'political' theologians.

For some Catholic theologians, these analyses of the major existential questions disclosed in the shifting cultural (and thereby basic existential) 'situations' of Christian reflection may seem culturally but not really theologically important. For however much some Catholic theologians may disagree with the specifics of Karl Barth's theology, they share his challenging assault upon *all* theologies articulating situational questions before interpreting the kerygmatic response. In Barth's own resounding words, 'Revelation is hurled at man like a stone'.

For most Catholic theologians, however, the main-line Catholic tradition on the relationship of faith and reason would incline them to agree, *caeteris paribus*, with Paul Tillich's observation on Barth's comments: 'Men do not receive answers to questions they have never asked'. Revelation, to be sure, should transform not only our answers but our questions. Yet it seems an unhappy commentary upon the transformative possibilities of Christian revelation to suggest, in effect, that the question 'Why did God make us' is not as situation-dependant a question as any other in the history of Christian thought.

A curious *hiatus* in Catholic scholarship tends to render any analysis of the situation on the traditional Catholic catechetical question and answer more difficult than most similar analyses. For it seems fair to observe that although there exist several excellent Catholic historical-hermeneutical studies of the *ethos*-situation of the New Testament period, the patristic and medieval periods, the Reformation period, individual situations within the Catholic post-Tridentine, pre-Vatican II period (e.g., Aubert's several works, the work on Tübingen, on Newman, on Pascal, or Pottmeyer's ground-breaking work on Vatican I), and many fine analyses of the changing 'questions' of the Vatican II and post-Vatican II periods, we still seem to lack not historico-empirical analyses but 'ethos' analyses for the 'situations' formative for the main-line Catholic question and answer in the several catechisms of the post-Tridentine, pre-Vatican II period.

Certain features of that 'situation' do, however, seem reasonably clear: the question 'Why did God make us?', unlike the questions disclosed in the biblical, patristic, medieval or post-Vatican II periods, cannot but strike one as relatively unexistential compared to such questions as mortality, harmony, forgiveness, meaning. In one sense, of course, that catechetical question could serve as a formulation of any of the questions listed above. And yet, the more strictly intellectualist cast of the question suggests a situation of relative security from the confusions and ambiguities in existence suggested by the other 'situational' questions. That formulation of the question also suggests a rather secure world of Christendom in which clear, distinct and, in their manner, admirably straightforward questions receive equally clear and distinct answers. It does not suggest a highly troubled world of anxious searchers for meaning and truth restlessly struggling, like Augustine in late antiquity or Karl Rahner in our own period to find the appropriate way to formulate a question really resonant to our experience of the radical ambiguity of all existence so that a response of revelation at once confrontational and healing might perform its properly transformative task. As such, revelation transforms both our everyday questions and the usual, sometimes lacklustre, sometimes brilliant but finally unsatisfactory answers grounded in our own resources.

When one turns for an analysis of the catechetical question to its usual answer 'To know, love, and serve Him in this world and to be happy with Him for all eternity in the world to come', one finds further clues to the *ethos* of the 'situation' and thereby to the major resources in the tradition appealed to for these purposes. The first features of this answer which commands respect are its clarity and directness. Like the question to which it responds the answer discloses a world of assurance in the faith as well as a clarity about the faith which we moderns, sometimes with slightly grudging admiration, sometimes with somewhat nostalgic regret, cannot but respect. Yet we also know that this answer does not really respond in a transformative manner to the post-Cartesian sense of radical ambiguity in our personal existence or the post-Marxist sense of alienation and oppression in our social existence. Without arrogance, yet without regrets, we know that this question and this answer cannot suffice for our situation, any more than Justin Martyr's response could suffice for Augustine.

PERSPECTIVES OF A BROADER ANSWER

A second feature of the traditional answer, however, may well strike us as kerygmatic in the best sense: indeed, as representative of the core of the tradition at its best. For who can doubt when reading this response (to know, love and serve God) that it has a radically theocentric character? Moreover, the very genre of the catechism, which forces a recognition of an addressee who asks questions, frees even the *quoad se* character of the Scholastic doctrine of God to have a more *quoad nos* formulation. For we, the questioners, are clearly made to understand that the Christian message is not merely a message of consolation or information. Rather God—and God alone—is the fundamental reality of our existence. If we really appropriate this truth of all truths, then we cannot but resolve to demand of ourselves the highest demand—to know, love and serve this God in this life. It remains true, to be sure, that the question of God is not here as radically posed as the question of the very meaning of our existence—as it was for Origen, Augustine, Thomas, Pascal, Newman and most contemporary theologians. Yet the radical theocentrism of the answer and the command-demand prescriptive aspect (know, love, serve) present in the description of discipleship remain to challenge any too easy attempt at allowing even the most radical experience of the situation determine the reality of God. In more technical theological language, it may well be true that the drive to *quoad se* language for God tended to obscure the radically anthropological *quoad nos* character of our fundamental existential question of God. As such the traditional response tends to allow that question to remain unformulated. It thereby obscures, in spite of all its too highly purchased clarity, the radically existential character of the question itself and the radical trust in God and loyalty to God's cause of love which should define Christian faith as 'belief-in' God, prior to all 'beliefs-that' God exists, has these attributes, and so on.

However, the unguarded and somehow untroubled nature of the radical theocentrism of the traditional response may serve as a challenge to our own attempts at formulation. For the intensity of the crisis of meaning for us moderns has so influenced our ability to ask fundamental questions that we are constantly tempted—even in our theologies— to develop profoundly existential anthropologies without an equally profound *theo*-logy. Just as the Catholic tradition at its best has always encouraged a radical doctrine of sin provided that the doctrine of grace be equally radical, so too the 'old answer' of the catechism may serve to remind us that however radical the existential, personal questions in the 'situation', still the Christian faith discloses a yet more radical answer—the reality of God and thereby the fundamental trustworthiness of reality itself whose final word is the God who is love. That answer challenges and transforms all our usual questions and answers.

It is also true that the theocentrism of this traditional answer lacks a Christocentric focus. As the Reformed tradition in theology has taught us and as almost every major contemporary Catholic theologian would insist, a theocentrism not allied with a Christocentrism (the latter not necessarily of an exclusivist kind) will not do. For it does not speak to the heart of the biblical revelation that God has decisively revealed himself in the event-gift of Jesus the Christ. This familiar objection is undoubtedly an important one. And yet, as the scholastics might say, *debemus distinguere*. Any specific question-answer in any catechism must be seen in the context of the genre as a whole. If the whole does not bear a Christocentric character, then the parts cannot supply it.

Just as we now know that Aquinas' *Summa* cannot fairly be accused of a lack of Christocentrism because the radically theocentric character of the first two parts become radically Christocentric only in Part Three, so the traditional catechisms—lacking, to be sure, the genius of the *exitus-reditus* schema of Aquinas' genre for the *Summa*—do possess a more modest genre disclosing a schema that, on the whole, is genuinely Christocentric.

Nevertheless, this fair-minded apologia for the catechism here (or, for that matter, for the structure of Aquinas' *Summa*) should not obscure the fact that an authentically Christian response to the question of the meaning of our lives must bear a radically anthropocentric-Christocentric-theocentric character if it is to be faithful to the all-compassing complexity and resonant and transformative power of the Christian kerygma itself. For this very reason—which, let us note, is not so much a reason developed from the questions of our situation as it is a reason demanded by the reality of the kerygma itself—the traditional answer does not suffice but demands an answer where the reality of Jesus Christ is present explicitly and decisively at every moment.

My reflections now come to the final phrase of the old answer 'and to be happy with Him in the world to come'. Since Vatican II, all Catholic Christians have become concerned about, and sometimes alarmed at, any move to an exclusively 'other-worldly' spirituality. It seems unfair to charge this final famous phrase of the old catechism with this weighty accusation. The conjunction 'and' does not mean 'in order to' so that any unhappy flight from this—worldly responsibilities should not be charged to this cathecatical account. Moreover, since a firm belief in eternal life remains a central affirmation of Catholic Christianity there also seems no good reason to disallow the explicit articulation of this belief and its attendant spirituality.

Still, exact meaning is one thing and the emphasis of the use of that meaning is quite another. Insofar as the famous final phrase of the old Catholic catechism does encourage a lessening of the sense of responsibility for this world of time and history or a subtle move to egocentricity of concern for my rewards in 'the world to come' away from the radical theocentricity and theocentric sense of responsibility in the answer as a whole, that phrase too should be reformulated. To insist on the belief in eternal life as a central proposition of the Catholic faith seems entirely appropriate. To formulate that belief in such manner that no single person will be tempted by the wording to retreat from this-wordly responsibility or egocentric concern seems entirely appropriate as part of the demand which our authentic questions in our situation impose upon us.

If these theological reflections upon the 'old' Catholic answer are at all accurate, then two clear conclusions follow: first, the old answer as faithful to its situation, as theocentric in its answer and Christocentric and responsible in the context of the genre 'catechism' as a whole functioned as a responsible response to the age-old question of the meaning of our existence; second, the very shift in our existential situation united to the more Christocentric and this-worldly understanding of the heart of the Christian kerygma demands a more appropriate question and answer for this latter day.

Antonio Plamadeala

An Orthodox Answer

THE QUESTION is an ever-relevant one. Even if one could lay one's hands on hundreds of treatises by the best authorities, all giving their replies, the question would still be asked all the time by everyone, and everyone would look for his own reply. The history of human culture in general, and of philosophy in particular, show a variety of replies with the greatest possible degree of variation between them. There is a whole spectrum ranging from the pragmatic, earthly aim of Confucianism, for example, through life as liberation from life and entry into 'Nirvana' or life as a means of obtaining happiness in the paradise of the Prophet, to the qualitative leap of Christianity, whose aim is becoming like the Most High—deification.

The believer looks to his religion for his reply. The mature Christian turns to the Scriptures, or inherits his from tradition. But his first contact with the reply is an earlier one, dating from the first moment his mind finds itself coming to grips with the question. Then it is the catechism that tells him what he should believe about the end of his life on earth. For many, though not for all, the reply they find in the catechism is the one that holds good for the rest of their life. This is why it is worth seeing what the catechism has to say on the subject, in the past and today.

Does it say something different today from what it said in the past? Was the catechism answer in the past conditioned by situations that no longer obtain today, or was it formulated independently, so that it was uninfluenced by particular situations and there is no distinction to be made between 'yesterday' and today? Or, if it was conditioned in the past, and the reply is different today, in what way is it different, and to what extent is it an improvement on what went before?

THE TRADITIONAL REPLY

These questions require some investigation, so let us look at some of the catechisms issued by the Romanian Orthodox Church.

The *Manual de chatehism al omului crestin si social* (Catechetical manual for Christian and social man) published in Bucharest in 1840 gives the following:

Q. For what object did God make man?

A. To be happy in himself in this world and in the next so that the power of God should thereby be glorified.

Q. What does man's true happiness consist in?

A. In the peace and tranquility of his soul: when a man examines his actions and finds that he has done no evil but has done good in all things, and therefore expects from God the reward he merits in this world and in the world to come.

Q. What must man do to merit the happiness for which he was created?

A. Apply himself with all his strength to carrying out three sorts of duty: toward God, toward himself and toward his fellow men.

I have quoted these questions and replies in full, because I shall return to them when I come to evaluate the various replies.

Other catechisms dispatch the question more briefly, giving shorter, simpler, and sometimes more abstract replies. Here is an example from 1853:

God created men for them to know him, honour him, adore him, glorify him and for them to obey him and be happy.[1]

Other Catechisms published in 1857, 1860, 1887 and 1915 give virtually identical answers:

The Omnipotent God has created man for man to know God, glorify him, love him, praise him and adore him and thereby obtain eternal life.[2]

The 1873 Catechism does not ask the question directly, but still provides an answer: we exist on earth in order to 'spend this fleeting life here below in peace, tranquility and happiness and so as to make us worthy to enjoy eternal happiness in the kingdom of heaven'.[3]

The 1892 catechism includes one or two additional ideas:

God has created man for him to be lord and master of all things and all the beasts of this world, so that he may use them to perfect himself, to know the Creator of all this, and to be happy.[4]

In general, this first group of catechisms, all dating from the last century, relates creation and its end to God on the one hand, to the gratitude, love, praise and honour man owes to God; and, on the other, to man, to his happiness here below and above all in the beyond if he carries out all his duties toward God—and only if he does so. Yet, as we have seen, the 1892 catechism does include the extra notion—a biblical one, too—that man has been created in order to dominate the rest of creation here on Earth, to govern it and use it, to perfect it and thereby perfect himself. It is true that he is to do all this in order to know God, but it still hints at the great philosophical concept of the postulation of 'knowledge'. It is realistic, also, in the way it sets man the objective of making the world *progress*, and of progressing in self-knowledge at the same time, the two progressions even being seen as dependent on each other. This is a balanced doctrine, far from the abstractions of some other catechisms, as from the excess of those mystical currents of thought that demand total abandonment of worldly goods and man's exclusive consecration of himself to his spiritual perfectioning through solitude and prayer.

The first catechism we considered—the 1840 one—displays the same balance: God created us for us to work out our own happiness, on Earth as well as in heaven. If we can achieve this, God, our creator, will thereby be glorified. The guide for our deeds is our conscience in the first place—a directly accessible earthly guide—which can either bring us peace and tranquileity of mind or not. But the signs that tell us if we are on the right road come not only from our conscience, but also from God who rewards us, not only in heaven, but also here below. Finally, the happiness for which man was created is not to be obtained by detachment, by relationship with God alone through a theoretical faith, but through good works.

The 1840 catechism gives a firm indication of the duties that man has to carry out equally in three directions: 'towards' God, towards himself and toward his neighbours'. His duties toward his neighbours, so to society, to the world and all this term implies, are expressely pointed out.

In the nineteenth century, Romanian spirituality was deeply influenced by the Païsien school. Païsie Velitchicovski, abbot of the monastery of Neamţ, had just died in 1794, having re-kindled a broad Hesychastic current in Romania spirituality, centred on 'the prayer of the heart', fulfilment and deification, in the truest Palamite tradition. All the great Fathers of prayer—St Gregory of Palamos, Simeon the New Thelogian, Isaac the Syrian, John Climacus, Ephraim the Syrian and others—were translated into Romanian at this time and as much was written on the subject in the space of a few years as had been in the previous century, as a mass of manuscripts and printed works of the period testify to this day. One would have expected Païsienism to put its stamp on the life of the people on the level of religious instruction of the masses, of the young, and on the normal catechesis of the Church, but there is no evidence of this. On the contrary, the catechisms put as much stress on this world as on the next.

Furthermore, the Romanians immediately set about correcting Païsie in his very spirituality, and his disciples such as Abbot Gheorghe, Metropolitan Gregory Dascălul, and later St Celinic of Cernica, founded a new school of specifically Romanian spirituality more attuned to the native mentality. This was the school of Cernica,[5] which stressed work, the ministry of service, even of social service—works of benefaction and charity—and prayer at the same time.

Païsienism took root in nineteenth-century Russia more easily than in Romania; his Hesychastic manuscripts had been translated into Russian, and soon became widespread, giving rise to the so-called 'Startsi' school or movement, which also embraced lay people, such as Dostoievski, Leontiev, and so on.

Two nineteenth-century Russian catechisms, also issued in Romanian, give a more laconic reply to the question under discussion, one that might be called more Païsien in spirit than those given in the native Romanian ones. So, for example, the *Catechism* of Filaret of Moscow says this: God made man so that man might come to know God, to love him, adore him, and so be eternally happy'.[6] The catechism published by Anthony of Kiev gives virtually the same reply:

Q. To what end did God create man?
A. So that man might know God, love him, glorify him, and thereby receive eternal happiness.[7]

The Romanians have often translated works by their Orthodox neighbours, but have not allowed themselves to be dominated by their excesses—when they have been carried away by excess. They have always operated a sort of local filter to hold a balance between strictly spiritual concern directed to man's fulfilment and salvation, and his social activity, the carrying-out of his more mundane earthly tasks. The faithful, and the priests too, for that matter, have always taken a realistic, rather than a unilateralistic, attitude to the answers. For example, a Romanian translation of the *Catechism* by Diomedes Kyriakos was issued, laying unilateral stress on the aim of spiritual fulfilment, achievement, of becoming like God through union with God, and identifying happiness with this spiritual fulfilment, which should relate only to contemplation of God, to *theosis*, as in purest Palamism:

> So, being united to God, man finds the fulfilment of his highest spiritual desires in him, as in the most perfect being. This is the highest destiny of man. Every man should aspire to this destiny, and should also desire and help his neighbours to strive toward this destiny.[8]

This answer, while enthusiastically received in the monasteries and among those with the deepest spiritual preoccupations, did not appear to worry the simple faithful, the average Christians in the street, who kept their peace of mind by choosing a more modest way, expressed in carrying out their elementary duties toward God, themselves and society.

Naturally, no Orthodox could say that man's destiny is not his spiritual fulfilment, his perfection, *theosis:* the Hesychast logic is irrefutable and prescribes the summits of the glory man can reach through ascesis, *hesychia* and prayer. This is the ideal for the elite, the perfect, the ascetics. But to answer simple catechism questions in this style, which means answering the questions asked by the ordinary people who do not spend their lives in monasteries or hermitages, but who live in society, learn a trade, carry out materialistic, hard tasks, work for their daily bread and to keep their families—this is to give them an answer that does not mean very much to them, that is not meant for them, is too pretentious and too specialized, however true. Not all Orthodox are Hesychasts!

One remark to avoid a possible misunderstanding: to distinguish between 'simple faithful' and 'Hesychasts' does not imply excluding the former from the unutterable joys of the kingdom of Heaven, from deification and contemplation, from *theosis*. The ways of the Lord are many and the means to him are not only those laid down in the rule-books, however well-tried these may be. The heights can also be reached by the common way of carrying out one's duties conscientiously, fearing God, bringing up children and placing oneself at the service of society. Orthodoxy has never sanctioned, encouraged or practised an absolute separation between those who follow the high road to God and those who take the low road of daily life.

THE PRESENT

Closer to our own time, in the conditions of modern life, the catechism[9] issued by Metropolitan Irineu Mihălcescu, like earlier Romanian catechisms, stresses man's duties toward his life here below as much as those that concern his eternal destiny. A *Confession of Faith*[10] published by the Holy Synod of 1952 adds this: 'Through his body, man is linked to humanity and the world; through his soul, he is linked to God'.

Other similar Romanian catechisms contain the notion—common to all dogmatic treatises as well—that man was initially created 'in order to share in the joy of being close to God'. At the time of the creation, God did not envisage the fall, and the human ends of man's life on earth. This is not the place for theological discussion of this point, since the question at issue concerns the purpose of man's life on earth after the fall, in a state of sin. Nevertheless, it is worth remarking that many catechisms—and not only the Orthodox—make no distinction between life in paradise and life on earth after the fall, and equate the question 'What are we here for?' with 'Why did God create man?'.[11]

This equation perhaps gives rise to some confusion between writer and reader: some writers are envisaging the creation of man and his original state in paradise when they formulate their answer, whereas their readers assume it applies to man's state on earth after his fall from grace. The authors should make their purpose clearer. It is perhaps this confusion that underlies the different purposes stressed, and the different levels of aim laid down. Clearly, the aim set for Adam in paradise was total spiritual fulfilment and life next to God in contemplation— somewhat more easily attainable in the conditions he knew. But the situation has changed, and men on earth now have other means at their disposal, varying with the various circumstances in which they live their lives. Contemplation is now the preserve of certain choice spirits, isolated and specialized—if the word is not too harsh in a spiritual context.

Orthodox Christians, however, will find the confusion only on paper, having the good sense to approach life and its purpose in a spirit of realism.

The *Orthodox Christian Catechism*[12] published at Arad in Rumania in 1957 no longer asks the question: What are we here for? (nor do the classic Orthodox *Confessions*), but after answering the question: 'What sort of laws governed man's life in Paradise?' (and answering: the law of labour, of domination of nature, the law of his development and perfectioning by means of language, spirit and culture, the law of bodily purity, of free will and of obedience to God), concludes that the same laws also govern man's life on earth 'of which he has been appointed master': so the undertaking of work is normal and comes from God, as does involvement in everything natural, out of obedience to God's commandments.

The task of formulating a catechism reply that would be 'characteristic of our time' has not been undertaken, because, as we have seen, the old answers are still valid. Their formulation may be laconic, but they are at least precise and condensed; they give indications and a general line of direction which in our case has not changed. The world the Orthodox Church lives in today has asked it to play a part in the life of society, but not a bigger part than in the past, and the Church has not felt itself called to do other than it always has done. But I should not generalize; this may be particularly true of the Romanian Orthodox Church and of Romania as a whole, where the Church has always been close to the people, a Church of the people. This is not said to designate its activity in the life of the nation, though it plays its part, but to show the realism of its integration in the daily life of the community, in both the spiritual and physical life of the faithful. The clergy contributed to the creation, development and unification of the language and to the birth of Romanian culture. Members of the clergy have stood beside the peasants in their uprisings, have been educators and fathers of families, have shared the life of the people. Through all this, the social dimension has been present in the Church's catechesis. When the Patriarch Justinian called the new orientation he proposed to his clergy in the changing conditions of the post-war years a 'social apostolate', he was only giving a fine new name to what the Orthodox Church had been doing throughout its history: it had always been a servant Church.

The norms governing its catechetics were imposed on its life by a sort of dynamic and realistic fusion between the religious life and daily life in society. Our catechetical instruction is carried out through the divine services, through the sacraments, confession in particular, through direct contact between priest and people, and between people and the dynamic movement of the seasons of the year with their feasts and blessings of daily activities, through special prayers such as those to bless a house, for a good harvest, and so on. No one looks on the catechism as a sort of pocket-book full of ready-made rules and answers to keep by one in case of trouble.

The catechisms give ideas—our first ideas—and because they are clear and precise, these ideas are also the last word on their subject. Simple answers are the best and the most lasting.

Our old catechisms helped the Orthodox faithful to find a happy medium between the things of the spirit and the things of this world. Till now, we have not felt the need to produce new ones, which does not mean that we should not: their language could be brouht up-to-date; they could be enlarged, perhaps, but basically they should say the same things as the old ones did.

Notes

1. Nifon Bălăşescu, *Catehismu Micu* . . . (The Little Catechism) (Iaşi, 1853).

2. *Katihisul Bisericii Rasaritului* (The Catechism of the Eastern Churches) (Buzău, 1860), p. 44; I. Stefanelli, *Invătătura crestinească a Bisericii ortodoxe* (The Christian teaching of the Orthodox Church) (Bucharest, 1887), p. 49; *Micul Catehism ortodox* (The Little Orthodox Catechism), compiled by Sofronie, Bishop of Rîmnic (Noul Severin, 1915), p. 253.

3. T. Codrescu, *Catehismul elementariu alu religiunei crestine* (Elementary Catechism of the Christian Religion) Iaşi, 1873), p. 4.

4. Economul St. Càlinescu, *Nou Catehismu ortodoxu* (New Orthodox Catechism) (Bucharest, 1892), p. 7.

5. Nicolae Serbănescu, '*Sfîntul ierarh Calinic de la Cernica*' (The Hierarch St Calinic of Cernica), in the review *Biserice Ortodoxă Română*, nos. 3–5, 1968), p. 353.

6. *Katihisul ortodoksu* (Orthodox Catechism), published by Meletie Istrati, Bishop of Husi (Iaşi, 1857), p. 44.

7. *Catehismul crestin ortodox* (Christian Orthodox Catechism), trans. Econom. I. P. Tincoca (Neamţu, 1925), p. 44.

8. A. Diomid Kyriacos, *Catehism crestin*, trans. Bishop Gherasim of Roman (Bucharest, 1900), p. 33.

9. I. Mihălcescu, *Catehismul crestinului ortodox* (Catechism of the Orthodox Christian) (Cernica, 1927), p. 5.

10. *Invătătura de credintă crestină ortodoxă* (The Teaching of the Orthodox Christian Faith) (Bucharest, 1952), p. 65.

11. See, e.g., *Christian Confession*, by Petru Movilă (1642), tran. into Rumanian (Bucharest[2], 1922), which states merely that God left man 'under the sway of his Spirit' (pp. 37–39). *Mărturisirea* (Confession, 1625), by Mitrofan Critopulos, merely says that God did not make men because he needed them, and the end of their sojourn on earth is related to banishment, repentance and redemption (latest Rumanian ed., Sibiu, 1973, trans. I. Icǎ); *idem. Invătătura crestină ortodoxă* (Timişoara, 1971), and 'Indreptar crestin ortodox' (Orthodox Christian Guide), in *Mitropolis Bantului* XXI (1971), nos. 4–6, pp. 211–44. All these see the creation of man as being 'for his happiness in being next to God, in loving him, knowing him and glorifying him' (p. 213).

12. Ilarion V. Felea, *Catehism crestin ortodox* (Arad, 1957), p. 20.

Translated by Paul Burns

Per Erik Persson

A Lutheran Answer

AS CAN be deduced from the article by Professor van de Poel, the preliminary question of the catechism discussed here manifests itself distinctly in both the Catholic and the Reformed traditions. However, it does not occur in Luther's Small Catechism of 1529, hence no examples will be taken from the Lutheran catechetical tradition. The *Evangelical Catechism for Adults* (1975) will only be included at the end of the article. I thus find myself in the somewhat curious situation of trying to give a 'Lutheran answer' to a question which does *not* seem to be a genuinely Lutheran question.

ORIGINS OF THE LUTHERAN CATECHISMS

Luther's catechisms, which both belong to the formal Lutheran creed (which to a certain extent explains their force of conviction) do not start with the kind of question normally encountered in the western Christian tradition. Instead, Luther simply proceeds from the ten commandments, followed by the 'Creed', the 'Our Father' and finally the sacraments of 'holy Baptism' and 'the altar'. The opening statement in the Small Catechism is the first commandment: 'Thou shalt not have other gods'. The first question posed is therefore the question as to the meaning of this commandment, presented in Luther's characteristic formulation: 'What is that?'.

The absence of the catechism question under discussion in the genuine Lutheran catechetical tradition also becomes apparent if we trace its development since the time of the Reformation. It would be impossible to follow every aspect of the catechetical tradition in the Lutheran Church or to grasp it comprehensively. Instead, I shall limit myself to observations about the situation in Scandinavian countries, in

particular Sweden. Here, Luther's Small Catechism played an instru-
mental rôle as the basis and focal point for religious instruction. Because of its summary character, it was however continually added to,
in the shape of more detailed 'catechism commentaries' officially ap-
proved by the church leaders in the various countries concerned. These
commentaries were conceived along the same lines as the Small
Catechism, as indeed were all official catechism interpretations authorized by the Swedish Church since the Reformation.[1] They have
appeared in countless editions, all following faithfully Luther's Small
Catechism—with one single exception. They all contain a preface,
which forms an introduction to the subsequent discussion of the five
'main sections'. The opening words of this introduction do not, as is the
case in the Small Catechism, consist of a quotation from the Bible, but
take the form of a question. In form and content, this question derives
from one of the first catechetical works written in Sweden during the
Reformation: the 'catechism' appended to the collection of sermons by
the Swedish reformer Olavus Petri, published in 1530.[2] The question
posed is: 'Why am I a Christian?'.[3]

For centuries this question was the introduction to instruction in the
Christian faith within the Swedish Church. It therefore fulfilled the
same function as the questions 'Why are we on this earth?' or 'Quelle
est la principale fin de la vie humaine?' in the Catholic or Reformed
traditions respectively. In the Danish and above all in the Norwegian
Churches (in the latter case almost exclusively so until the mid-
nineteenth century) E. Pontoppidan's pietistically orientated catechism, authorized in 1737, was used. Closely related to that of P. J.
Spener, it began with the question: 'Do you not wish to be happy on
earth and blessed in heaven?'. This is an approach very similar to the
type of question characteristic of the Catholic and Reformed traditions.
However, this never became dominant in official catechetical statements of the Swedish Church. The importance of the opening question
is crucial, for it determines the direction of the whole catechism.

In our context it is especially interesting to note that the opening
question in the catechetical tradition of the Swedish Church (I shall
from now on refer only to that tradition) is not a question about what it
means to be a human being, but what it means to be a Christian. The
answer to this question consists of a directive concerning baptism,
formulated roughly as follows: 'I am a Christian, because through
baptism I have been received into the community of Jesus Christ and
with the community I believe and profess that he is my Saviour and
Redeemer'. This leads shortly to a question about where one is to seek
instruction in the meaning of the Christian faith, the answer being 'the
Bible', which in turn consists of 'the Law and the Gospel'. From this

point on, the Swedish catechism concurs with Luther, moving straight on to the 'Ten Commandments of God'. These are characterized as a 'short summary of the Law'. In conclusion, the 'articles of faith' are presented consecutively as a 'summary of the Gospel'. This division into 'Law' and 'Gospel' is a consistent tendency in the Lutheran catechetical tradition.

THE LAW AND THE CHRISTIAN LIFE

On the question of 'the Christian life' there is a conflict between the opening statements of the Swedish catechism and Luther's catechisms, which attempt to interpret and define this concept. For Luther, the 'law' is not something specifically 'Christian', but an expression of 'humanity'. The decalogue is only one of many expressions of the 'natural law' by means of which God guides all men and all creation— not just Christians. It is the basis of all human co-existence on this earth and is given practical expression in the multiplicity of orders and offices instituted by God, determined solely by the fact that they promote work which is of service to other people.[4] Through his Law, which is thus by no means confined exclusively to the Bible, God perserves the world he has created from the permanent threat of destruction by the forces of evil.

With the decalogue, the first important section of the catechism, one is not introduced to the Church as such, but to the many-sided earthly reality in which every human being—and hence the Christian too—finds himself. The starting point is not the question of how to achieve 'blessedness' but rather the social context in which everyone has a fellow man, a 'neighbour'. It is concerned with 'communal daily tasks in which a man may act against his neighbour'.[5] This does not refer to another world, but to this one, in which God gives each and every man his own historical task to fulfil. Everything is enveloped in the Law of God, which in its 'social' or 'political' manifestations urges men to work and action. This 'first section of Christian doctrine' encompasses 'everything that God wishes us to do and not do' and 'one should have one's hands full of things to do here'.[6] Here, too, we find what seems to be at least a partial answer to the question 'Why are we on this earth?' when we read: 'that I . . . may keep his commandments'. But this is *not* followed by 'in order that after death I may be counted among the blessed in heaven'.[7] Instead, we read: 'so that I may serve my fellow men'.

However, men do not regard these actions inspired by God as being directed towards their fellow men. Instead, they regard their deeds as a means of justifying themselves in the eyes of God and earning a place

in heaven. The confrontation with this 'justification of work' consti-
tutes a distortion and misuse of God's Law, which thereby acquires a
new (spiritual' function; the Holy Spirit uses the Law as a means of
accusation and it becomes a trial of conscience in men's minds. Man's
confidence in his own actions proves to be without foundation since he
has not in fact fulfilled the demands of the Law. Hence he stands before
God as a sinner and justifiably condemned.

The 'first section' is followed by 'the creed, which describes everything we may expect to receive from God', and this is 'a very different
doctrine to the ten commandments. For they define what we should do,
whereas this creed states what God does and gives'. The creed is not
concerned with demands and stipulations, but with 'mercy'.[8] Here the
concern is not with 'the human codition' in general, but with the 'life of
the Christian', for 'these articles of faith separate us Christians from all
other people on earth'.[9] What we encounter at this point is the Gospel,
rather than the law; the benificence shown us by the Trinity, centred
upon the discussion about Jesus Christ in the second article of faith.
This in turn is concerned not with what we give, but with what we
receive: 'that God created me together with all other creatures', 'that
Jesus Christ . . . is my Lord who has redeemed me from perdition
and damnation', 'that . . . the Holy Spirit has summoned me through
the Gospel'.[10]

This Gospel of God's incomprehensible love and mercy towards
sinners who have justifiably earned salvation is *specifically Christian*.
Both the Law and the Gospel are certainly 'the word of God' but they
have different functions. By means of the Law, we are urged to perform
deeds in the service of others; at the same time it tries and passes
judgment on every human being if he does not keep God's commandments and fulfil its demands. The Gospel, on the other hand, imparts
the only justification that is valid in the eyes of God, which in Reformation terminology is summarized as 'the forgiveness of sins'. This is not
something we do, but something promised by God which can only be
received by believing in his Word.

LAW AND GOSPEL

The *conflict* indicated above between 'Law' and 'Gospel' is charcterisi-
tic of Luther and the Lutheran tradition. Through the Law, God effects
the opposite to what he does through the Gospel: the Law accuses and
condemns, whereas the Gospel acquits and consoles; the Law makes
demands and claims, whereas the Gospel gives and bestows. This curious duality is echoed in anthropological terminology, when we find the

Christian described as simultaneously 'old' and 'new', *simul peccator et iustus*. As the 'old' man and sinner he is subject to the Law like all other men: throughout his earthly life he is bound by duty to pray daily, 'forgive us our trespasses'. But as the 'new' and 'acquitted' man he lives in the belief that sins will be forgiven, as stated in the Gospel. At the heart of this 'conflict' there is a profound connection between the two; for both Law and Gospel constitute the Word of God, through which God carries out his actions on earth. In the same way, for a Christian acceptance of the Law is linked with forgiveness—for only the person condemned to death can truly understand what is meant by mercy.

The profound significance of this simultaneous conflict and homogeneity is demonstrated with incomparable clarity and distinctness in the explanation of baptism in Luther's catechism. The answer in the Small Catechism to the question 'What is the meaning of baptism by water?' is as follows (with reference to Rom 6): 'It means that the old Adam in us should be drowned by daily repentance and penance and die with all sins and evil desires, so that a new man may arise each day, living constantly in justice and purity for the sake of God'.[11] And in the Greater Catechism it is stated that 'the power and strength' of baptism is 'nothing more than the death of the old Adam, and the resurrection of the new man, who would both exist within us for the rest of our lives; hence a Christian life is simply a daily baptism which, once commenced, continues always'.[12]

Here the conflict is taken to the extreme and depicted as the fundamental contrast between 'dead' and 'alive'. It is concerned with nothing less than union with Christ himself, through his death and resurrection; in other words, with the central factor of the Gospel and of faith, namely the Easter event. In this way the 'homogeneity' is also made unequivocally clear. The man who rose from the dead is none other than the man who died on the cross. Hence to be a Christian means to abide by the Law of God as an 'old' man, to be crucified and suffer death daily, and remaining faithful to the Gospel of the Lord, to be reborn daily as a 'new' man and so become like Christ, who was crucified and rose from the dead. This life in the sign of Easter continues until death, when the 'old' man finally dies while the 'new' man lives 'eternally for God' by means of the resurrection on the day of judgment. Hence the 'conflict' belongs to this world; God's last and final word will be the Gospel which will overcome the Law, thus opening the way to a future without sin and death. *The* 'Lutheran answer' to the question 'Why are we on this earth?' can thus be formulated as follows: 'in order that we become like Christ, who was crucified and rose from the dead for our sake'.

LIFE IN THE CHRISTIAN COMMUNITY

In this context two aspects of this 'Lutheran answer' should be especially emphasized. Firstly, it expresses an attitude to life which includes an interpretation of the most difficult thing each man has to bear; his own suffering and death. Seen in the light of baptism and in the light of Easter, this is nothing less than union with Christ. Everything we do thus becomes a participation in Christ's crucifixion and can be interpreted with reference to his life. The effort needed to carry out tasks which demand that we give up our egoism instead of doing something useful for those around us; the set-backs which destroy all our hopes; the gnawing of our conscience at our own lack of charity; and finally, the decay of the body in death. For the desired image to emerge—in this case the image of Christ—the sculptor (God) must chip one piece after the other off the block of stone on which he is working. When the doctor cuts open a boil it burns painfully, but it is precisely this pain which brings with it health and life. When the 'old' man receives one death blow after the other, the 'new' man is thereby formed and the image of Christ emerges. Seen in the light of Easter, the hardships of life can be borne without bitterness; what appears to be meaningless is interpreted as signifying union with Christ. Hence one can sing a hymn of praise even in the midst of the deepest suffering—following the example of Paul and Silas in the prison at Philippi (Acts 16:25).

The other aspect which should be emphasized in this context is that the profound union with Christ referred to here is by no means something confined exclusively or primarily to the 'Church'. Symptomatic of this is Luther's linguistic innovation which consisted of extending the word 'vocation', *vocatio* (formerly used to denote the 'clergy' to describe *all* callings and tasks a Christian might perform in the service of others. It is precisely through this 'calling' or 'vocation' in all the different types of work and 'worldly' tasks that a Christian shares in the cross and assumes the image of Christ who was in this world 'for others'. Through church worship we participate in Christ be means of the sacraments and the word of the Gospel, which interprets our faith and gives meaning to human existence as the community of Christ. Hence to be a 'Christian' is not inferior or superior to 'human existence' but invests it with special meaning and significance in the widest possible sense.

I referred earlier to the conflict between Luther's choice of the decalogue as his starting point, i.e. 'human existence', and the Swedish catechetical tradition of beginning with the question about what it means to be a 'Christian'. The risk of the latter approach is there is a tendency to see the 'Church' as a community separate from the rest of human life. The answer to the question 'Why am I a Christian?' rightly refers to baptism which—if its content is implicitly expounded in Luther's catechisms—amounts to an interpretation which includes the daily toil of work on this earth in service of one's fellow men.

CRITICISM OF THE CATECHISM ANSWER

'The Lutheran answer', as briefly outlined above, implies simultaneously a critical attitude towards the type of answer usually found in the Catholic and Reformed traditions. So, in conclusion, I shall give an indication of the critical questions concerned. If the answers presented by these traditions refer so frequently, in fact almost continually, to *what man should do* in order to achieve eternal life (e.g., 'that I may know him, love him and keep his commandments') there is a real danger that the meaning of life will be interpreted as something we can achieve through our own efforts. How then could it have any meaning for the person who is not able to do what is demanded as the prerequisite for eternal life? Given the Lutheran starting-point, this type of answer reveals itself as a subtle form of self-justification whereby, instead of placing his trust in *what God gives*, the individual relies on his own pious works. And when the answer takes the form: 'in order to serve God and thereby find happiness in this world and in the next',[13] does this give a meaning to all negative experiences of suffering, guilt and conflict, which in reality constitute our lives both as human beings and as Christians? Both types of answer are stamped by an 'individualistic attitude to faith' (one might even describe it as 'salvation egotism') which disregards both our fellow men and the social dimension of human life. There is something strange about a 'Christian' answer which makes no specific mention of the Christian approach—the basic trust in Jesus Christ given us by God regardless of our achievements.

Nowadays, to give a relevant Christian answer to the meaning of human life is a pre-eminently ecumenical task. Curiously enough, the three elements which according to Yves Congar are lacking in the 'classical answer' are to be found in the 'Lutheran answer' as outlined above with reference to Luther's catechism. These elements are: 1. 'a social dimension'; 2. 'emphasis on our earthly and historical task'; and, above all, 3. 'a Christological orientation'.[14] But this is not my only reason for believing that this 'Lutheran answer' can make a noteworthy contribution to ecumenical discussions. I am also convinced that it is deeply rooted in the message of the Bible and in Christian experience. The critical point of the answer affects even those Churches which profess the 'Lutheran tradition'.

Notes

1. The so-called *Svebilius katekes* (1689; author Archbishop O. Svebilius); *Lindbloms katekes* (1810; a reworked, revised edition of the *Svebilius Catechism* by Archbishop J. A. Lindblom); *1878 års katekesutveckling* (catechical declaration of 1878; the outcome of a committee). Cf. also E. Lilja, *Den svenska katekestraditionen mellan Svebilius och Lindblom* (Stockholm, 1947), and N. Andersson, *1878 års katekes* (Lund, 1973).

2. Olavus Petri, *Een lijten postilla 1530* (most easily available in *Samlade skrifter av Olavus Petri*, III, p. 425 ff (Uppsala, 1916).

3. With the exception of the 1810 version revised and authorized by J. A. Lindblom, which instead begins with the question: 'What is the catechism?.

4. With reference to this and any subsequent comments about Luther, cf. especially G. Wingren, *Luthers Lehre vom Beruf* (Munich, 1952); *Luthers lära om kallelsen* (Lund,[2] 1948); *The Christian's Calling* (Edinburgh, 1957); *Luther on Vocation* (Philadelphia, 1957).

5. *The Great Catechism*, quoted from *The Formal Creeds of the Evangelical-Lutheran Church* (Göttingen,[2] 1952), p. 639.

6. Op. cit., pp. 646 and 639.

7. The formulation drawn up by Cardinal Gasparri in 1930; cf. H. Küng's article in this issue.

8. *Grosser Catechismus*, op. cit., pp. 646 and 661.

9. Op. cit. p. 661.

10. *Kleiner Catechismus*, op. cit. pp. 510–12.

11. Op. cit., p. 516.

12. Op. cit., p. 704.

13. The formulation of the Dutch Catechism of 1948, cf. F. van de Poel's article in this issue.

14. Cf. H. Küng's article in this issue.

Translated by Sarah Twohig

Gottfried Locher

A Reformed Answer

1. 'Why are we on this earth?' God knows. The Creator alone knows where we come from and what our destiny is; his knowledge is our destiny. He decrees where we go and our purpose in being. As saviour he carries this ordinance through, despite ourselves. *Dominus providebit*.

'Why are we on this earth?' According to classical Reformed doctrine the answer lies in the mystery of God. For our part, the answer lies in acknowledging our ignorance and inability to determine our lives and submitting to the Creator-saviour. This is not resignation, but an act of confidence, of trust, through which we are united mentally, spiritually and bodily with the spirit of God. And the trust which forgoes self-knowledge leads to knowledge of a higher order. It declares that the divine answer is good. We cannot explain it, yet we know we are in good hands, we are confidentially informed that we are needed in contexts of which we can have no conception, and that we have a meaningful task to fulfil.

'Why are we on this earth?' This we must learn from God. By learn, we mean the continuous, never-ending process of the formation of consciousness, repeatedly interrupted by set-backs and contradictory experiences. Throughout this process our knowledge and our understanding nevertheless always remain inferior to God's knowledge, and even to our own experiences. For only he can grasp the extent and implications of our existence, our deeds and our ommissions. Furthermore, we cannot manage to understand ourselves or our fellow men. We are notoriously unwilling to understand our eternal destiny, despite the fact that since time immemorial we have been questioning the purpose of our existence. We must know the answer.

2. This already establishes the fact that our question is always of an existential character. In other words, human existence depends totally on the answer. Whether this answer is reached theoretically or by practical means, without reflection, is of less importance than the theological considerations. The answer to the existential question is always arrived at by practical means, even when men theorize about it. One could, however, argue that only when conditions are favourable and men have sufficient leisure do they transform these fundamental questions about existence, such as 'Why are we on this earth?', into religion. Only then do they turn them into ethics, expand them into philosophy, use them as the basis for all knowledge; in other words, turn them into a theoretical problem. Yet all these aspects in effect always come back to the question of meaning. The resulting unrest, in western history at least, has manifested itself in all these ways, the forms of which have continually evolved, and always accompanied by the question of humanity. But whenever happiness is shattered, efforts fail, hope fades, trust is betrayed, even when inertia and indifference assert themselves, the question 'Why are we on this earth?' immediately becomes a dangerous one. On the brink of meaninglessness the existential question inevitably becomes more acute and reveals its dual nature: suggesting on the one hand that theoretical knowledge might be able to relieve need while at the same time doubting that such knowledge exists.

This has been so ever since men first tried to find an answer to the question of existence. We today are even less able to extricate ourselves from this dilemma than previous generations. For the knowledge of God which should lead us to find this meaning presupposes a kind of life and society that no longer exists. In addition, we are probably far more entangled in spiritual crises as a result of the threats and catastrophes of contemporary events than was ever the cases before 1914. We experience not only the destruction of countries, peoples and individuals, but also the vague threat that hangs over the whole world. The question of the meaning or meaninglessness of the cosmos is intimately linked with that of our own insignificant lives. The question of meaning becomes less and of less a theoretical question concerned with intellect or consciousness, and much more of a question of feeling or emotion. Ever since men realized that they have the means to destroy all life, no one feels safe in this world any more. The social and psychological consequences are obvious: almost simultaneously, in camps and torture chambers men are demonstrating what they are capable to doing to their fellow men. We are no longer safe, and our children will never be safe.

3. Bearing in mind that in the 'old answer' the question as to the purpose of existence led into the question of trust, its burning topicality cannot be denied. If we ask ourselves whether it is 'still adequate', the answer must be that it has by no menas been reached yet. Truth is, of course, not dependent on any given situation; but in a period of history characterized by a fundamental break-down of trust, Christianity is ideally suited to reveal a part of the knowledge of God which will help us to answer the question.

Anyone who does not have to answer or justify this fundemental 'why' will probably be shaken but not proved wrong by this radical approach. Much depends on the extent of his trust. In the face of outer and inner collapse, Christians know that they are specially summoned. In the age of Auschwitz, Hiroshima, Vietnam, Chile, 'Helsinki', they have much to do. Their service is needed. This is their good fortune, for whoever can help others will not find the world neaningless. By serving others the Christian is able to extend the meaning with which he has been endowed to those oppressed by doubt or despair. He faces our 'why?' with God's plan. 'Why are we on this earth?' The Christian perceives a deep-rooted connection between meaningfulness and meaninglessness in God's ways of dealing with mankind.

4. Theology tends to discuss these matters in the doctrine of 'providence' referred to above. Providence is connected to the divine teaching and precedes the fall and salvation. Hence sin is first and foremost conceived as the loss of meaningfulness. In contrast, whoever 'believes in God' discerns some recognizable structure in the confusion of events.

To perceive God in the world and to live a life dedicated to his glory; this is the 'supreme good'. So we read in the opening passages of Calvin's Geneva Catechism of 1542. He goes on to stipulate that the 'foundation' and 'principle' of trust in God is 'that we recognize him in Christ' (Jn 17:3).

The Heidelberg Catechism of 1563 applied this prinicple in a superlatively didactic fashion. With its closed way of thought and its pastoral approach this catechism became widely disseminated. Its doctrine of providence was a determining factor in Reformed piety. Indeed, it symbolized many of the pietistic movements. We have in mind here not the explicit treatment of providence (questions 26–8), but the famous first question, 'What is your only consolation in life and in death? That I . . . belong to Jesus Christ . . .', etc. In this context modern and 'sufficient' seems to presuppose a basic contradiction in meaning. In answer 26 the world is described as 'this vale of tears'. Hence the question of meaning or purpose 'Why are we . . .?') is never even posed, but is replaced by the question of salvation. This in turn yields its own answer: the existence of Jesus Christ and my belonging to him is the answer to this doubting 'why?'. To be more precise, it removes the threat and the fear from the question. Because of this the Catechism is then able (question 6) to take up the opening propositions of Leo Jud of Zürich and John Calvin of Geneva without causing the derision of the reader: 'God created man . . . according to His own image . . . that he might know and love God with all his heart, and live with Him in eternal bliss, praising and glorifying Him'. Whoever knows that he 'belongs to Christ' knows 'why he is on this earth'.

THE DOCTRINE OF PROVIDENCE AND ITS CRISIS

A systematic exposition of the Reformed doctrine of providence would not be appropriate here, for our theme is focussed on the crisis of piety. Hence I shall restrict my discussion to those aspects of the doctrine which relate to the question of meaning.

1. The *locus de providentia* insists that world and history are not meaningless. The concept of 'providence' is seldom mentioned in the Bible. It was taken from ancient philosophy, especially from the Stoa, where it fulfilled the same function. When it was absorbed into Christian theology it underwent a profound change. It is a very different matter to conceive of the cosmos as being governed by an impersonal universal law as against the all-powerful God of the Bible who conducts everything according to his purpose. If providence is understood in these terms it acquires universality validity. This can be seen explicitly, for example, in the earliest writings of the Old Testament, in the story of Joseph, in the Psalms and even—in dialectical form—in the Book of Job. The New Testament adopts it in a still more individual and intensive way; one need only think of Jesus' words about the sparrows, about the hairs on our heads, and the prayer heard by God even before we say it (Mt 6:8.32; 10:29ff.), as well as the passage in St Paul 'that in everything God works for good with those who love him' (Rom 8:28). A comprehensive survey would have to include at least the relationship between the church and the world in the Letter to the Colossians and the coming of the kingdom of heaven (Mk 13; 1 Cor 15; Acts).

2. Jesus' summons are directed towards his disciples; the doctrine of providence governing his destiny belongs also to his successors. The apostle, looking back on the Lord's death on the cross and ascension into heaven demands that we draw our own conclusions from the fact that in giving up his Son for us, the Father also undertook 'to give us all things with him' (Rom 8:32). At this point belief in providence becomes linked with belief in Christ, as is stressed by the reformers, especially Zwingli, and expressed in classical form in questions 26–8 of the Heidelberg Catechism. 'That the Father . . . for the sake of his Son

Jesus Christ is my God and my Father . . . he will fulfil every need of my body and my soul, and because he sent me into this vale of tears he will turn every evil to my advantage . . .' Since the Enlightenment the tenet of 'foresight' has frequently been in competition with that of salvation, and has even begun to encroach upon it. Here we have the opposite to the fall: belief in providence confirms belief in Christ. It provides the essential proof and justification of this regained innocence.

3. In the face of this tendency to centralize, the scholastic distinctions which have played a certain part in the reformed theology from Calvin through Schleiermacher to Karl Barth lose much of their relevance. For example, the *providentia generalis* and *specialis*, to which Abraham Kuyper added another *specialissima*; the *concursus* and *gubernatio*; the *causae secundae* taught by Calvin and the orthodox theologians, though not by Zwingli and Schleiermacher. The 'admission' of evil acquires a more active note in Reformed theology than it does in Lutheran teaching. It introduced the concept of discipline and propriety into religious life. The children of God do not acknowledge mere coincidence: everything comes to us 'not by chance, but from his paternal hand'. (HC 27).

4. But our central question ('still adequate') lays stress on the disputed problem as to whether providence manifests itself in each individual experience. Whoever raises the objection that faith is not an objective phenomenon should bear in mind that this in no way diminishes the reality of the articles of faith. A personal narrative certainly does not have the rational force of an argument, but it does possess the immediacy of a report. Once again, meaning is not proven, but is learned through experience. Now the evangelical faith does not rely on experience, but on the word. But this creates experience, indeed faith is already experience. One should occasionally be aware that God's ways are superior to ours (Isa 55:8f.) and that things work out for the best (Rom 8:28). As a rule the inner and the outer experience are in conflict and must accept the necessary strength offered.

5. The reason for this is that faith always remains linked to the cross. Only through faith can one learn how God's plan is concealed within Jesus' failure. According to God's providence it had to happen that way (Mk 8:31; Mt 26:54; Lk 24:26; etc.).

God's salvation was achieved through Christ's death on the cross, but the meaning of this act only manifested itself through its inherent blasphemous contradiction. So we too, in the world in which that happened, must always be ready to expect the enlightenment of Easter, contrary to the normal paths of reason.

6. Once again the 'old answer' has shifted the meaning into God's

mystery. Those who, disturbed by the meaninglessness of life, brought the news that 'God was dead' and focussed their attack on the theistic doctrine of providence, failed to consider the fundamental relationship between this doctrine and their own approach. Neither antitheism nor atheism can take men's godlessness so severely as a doctrine of providence based on the cross, which places all misery in the hands of God and trusts implicitly in God.

The verse 'Praise the Lord who guides all things in majesty' no longer seems tenable. Let anyone who disagrees cease to sing it! But when the poet Joachim Neander was dying of consumption at the age of twenty-nine he said that he would rather 'believe to death than die living'.

7. 'Since Auschwitz' providence is no longer valid, it has been said. In Auschwitz a rabbi was thrown into the latrine with a mocking taunt about what had become of his Jehovah, to which he replied: 'Here too is God'.

8. It must be admitted that the traditional form of piety based on providence is not able to cope with all aspects of the contemporary crisis. Even in the catechism it was often individualistic, often directed in a one-sided way towards the life hereafter, and often restricted to the devout people of God. We must learn from the Lord himself how providence expands to the dimensions of the kingdom.

The connection between Christian hope and the meaning of existence is presumably dealt with in another article.

THE PROBLEM OF AN ADEQUATE ANSWER

'Is the answer still adequate?' Yes and no.

1. Despite the objections and assertions implied by the 'still', the answer still remains, today and in the future.

2. Nevertheless, it is no accident that we have difficulty in understanding, adopting and passing on the old answer. The old answer and the new situation both make demands on our faith. In theological terms this means more pneumatology and more eschatology! In its Reformed version the doctrine of providence was too anchored on the first article, directed towards the creator and his eternal designs. This gave Reformed piety its steadfastness, but also often led to conservatism. The New Testament looks forward to the culmination far more than it does back towards the beginning.

This corresponds to the atmosphere of a stormy period of change. To a generation which departs from the precedent of thousands of years and seeks the meaning of its existence in the final aim rather than in the primal cause, Christianity may freely admit that it could have learned this from the biblical texts long ago. We must begin to describe providence as it relates to salvation. 'Why are we on this earth?'.

3. Every so-called 'old' answer might be right, and even helpful. But how could it ever be 'adequate'? For one answers the question as to the meaning of one's existence with one's whole life; through knowledge, love, service and worship. This, incidentally, is also advocated in the old text-books.

4. So long as men are filled with doubt at this 'why?', the Lord poses us the same question. We can never repeat an old answer to him. His question demands that each one of us take the effort to find personal formulations appropriate to the conditions of contemporary society. It is a never-ending process. We can never give a stock answer. Everything we do is either an answer or a refusal to answer.

5. 'Why are we on this earth?' God's majesty is the source of all our happiness. We believe in it. Sometimes we are moved by it. It will fulfil itself in spite of all misery. God poses us the question which silences us, and he himself causes the answer of certainty to sink into our souls. Thus no intellectual, social or linguistic restructuring, nor even a catastrophe, can alter it in any way. This answer remains adequate.

Appendix

From the Heidelberg Catechism of 1563:

Question 1: What is your sole consolation in life and in death? That I belong body and soul, in life and in death not to myself, but to my loving saviour Jesus Christ, who with his precious blood has paid for all my sins and freed me from the power of the devil, thus ensuring that unless it be the will of my Father who is in heaven, no hair may fall from my head, that everything should contribute to my happiness. Hence he also promises me eternal life, through his Holy Ghost and makes me truly ready and willing to live in him.

Question 6: Did God create man so evil and perverted? No, God created man good, just and holy, according to his own image, that he might know and love God with all his heart, and live with him in eternal bliss, praising and glorifying him.

Question 26: What do you believe when you say: I believe in God the Father, the Almighty, creator of heaven and earth? That the eternal Father of our lord Jesus Christ who created heaven and earth and everything in them out of nothing and upholds and governs everything through his eternal guidance and his providence is my God and Father, for the sake of his Son. In him I place my trust and have no fear that he will care for me in body and in soul, that he will even use the evil he imposes upon me in this vale of tears to my benefit. As the almighty God it is in his power to do so, and as my loving Father he wished to do so.

Question 27: What do you understand by God's providence? The almighty and eternally present power of God through which he upholds and governs heaven and earth and all creation. Foliage and grass, rain and drought, fruitful and unfruitful years, food and drink, health and sickness, riches and poverty—none of these things is the work of chance, for everything comes to us from his paternal hand.

Question 28: How does knowledge of the creation and God's providence help us? It gives us patience in our misfortune, gratitude in our fortune, and through our trust in God, our loving Father, the assurance for the future that no creature will separate us from his love, because he holds all creatures in his hand, so that nothing can stir or move without his will.

Translated by Sarah Twohig

Schubert Ogden

A Free-Church Answer

BECAUSE the task assigned to this essay is rather systematic than historical, I feel justified in restricting my attention to but one of the many answers that have in fact been given to the question, Why did God make me? in the traditions of the so-called Free Churches. One might feel all the more justified in doing this because, in the traditions of the English-speaking Free Churches, at least, there would appear to be extensive agreement in all essentials between their representative answers to this question. But be this as it may, it is in order to devote the available space to my assigned task of systematic theological assessment that the only Free-Church answer whose adequacy I shall attempt to assess is one given in my own tradition as a member of the United Methodist Church.

Before turning to this answer, however, we must briefly consider the criteria for assessing its adequacy, as well as the difficulties involved in applying these criteria. Speaking very generally, I should say that there are two such criteria (although I would not object to saying, instead, that there is a single two-fold criterion).

CRITERIA

In the first place, there is the criterion of *appropriateness to the Christian witness of faith,* by which I mean that no answer can be theologically adequate unless it expresses in its terms the same understanding of human existence that is already expressed in the terms of the constitutive and, therefore, normative witness of the Christian community. Of course, not the least difficulty in applying this criterion is that there is no consensus among Christians about just what is to be taken as normative Christian witness. Whereas for orthodox Protestants it is the witness of Scripture alone, for orthodox Roman Catholics it is the witness of Scripture and tradition, or of Scripture as interpreted by the teaching office of the Church, while for liberal Protestants it is the witness of the so-called historical Jesus. But an even more serious difficulty is that no witness can function as normative except by being interpreted and that nothing can guarantee the correctness of its interpretation. The risk inevitably remains in assessing the appropriateness of any answer that the norm of such assessment, whatever it is taken to be, will itself be misinterpreted.

Nor are these the only difficulties involved in assessing theological adequacy. For in the second place, there is the criterion of *understandability to human existence,* by which I mean that no answer can be theologically adequate unless it is also meaningful and true when judged by the relevant standards of meaning and truth given implicitly in our existence as human beings. Naturally, from the standpoint of Christian faith, to determine that an answer is appropriate to the Christian witness is to do enough to conclude that it is also meaningful and true and so understandable to human existence. But if what systematic theology has the task of determining is not only what Christians *believe* to be meaningful and true but what really *is* so, it clearly has to do more than determine the appropriateness of an answer in order to conclude to its understandability. And in trying to do this more theology is unavoidably faced with yet other difficulties, not the least of which is that there is no consensus among human beings about just what are to count as the standards for judging the meaning and truth of their various claims. In fact, if one works, as we certainly must today, against the horizon of *world* culture and history, the lack of agreement about such standards is apt to seem so great as to be overwhelming. Yet here, too, there is a further and still more intractable difficulty insofar as nothing can guarantee the correctness of any attempt to explicate the standards of meaning and truth that are given implicitly in our experience and understanding simply as human beings. For all we can ever know, even the most painstaking of such explications is itself meaningless or false in its formulation of those standards.

Our situation with respect to the task of assessing theological adequacy, then, seems to be this: although the two criteria for such assessment are, in general, clear enough and can be precisely formulated as, respectively, appropriateness to the Christian witness and understandability to human existence, the difficulties involved in any attempt to apply these criteria are such as to make the actual task of assessment anything but easy. And this becomes all the more evident as soon as we recognize that both criteria of adequacy necessarily have a variable as well as a constant aspect. Because theology is and must be as historically determined as anything else that human beings undertake to do, just what the general criteria of appropriateness and understandability require in a given case is always a function of the special historical situation in which the task of theological assessment can alone be carried out. What could have been assessed as appropriate yesterday may no longer be so today, and the same is true of what could have been previously judged to be understandable.

We have the best of reasons, therefore, for regarding the whole process of theological assessment—and that means, of course, the whole process of theology—as always unconcluded and inconclusive. This means, among other things, that we are fully justified in being concerned less with the conclusions of our assessments than with the warrants that entitle us to draw them. To take care to provide such warrants, and thus to clarify the conditions which, if fulfilled, entail the conclusions is about all that any of us can do individually to further the task of theological assessment.

WESLEY'S ANSWER

With this in mind, I turn directly to some teachings of John Wesley that are, in effect, his answer to the question, Why did God make me? Although these teachings are not set forth in the express form of a catechism, they leave no doubt that the question to which they are addressed is precisely this traditional catechetical question. Thus Wesley himself asks in one of his sermons, 'For what end is life bestowed upon the children of men? Why were we sent into the world?', only to reply:

> For one sole end, and for no other, to prepare for eternity. For this alone we live. For this, and no other purpose, is our life either given or continued. It pleased the all-wise God, at the season which he saw best, to arise in the greatness of his strength, and create the heavens and the earth, and all things that are therein. Having prepared all things for him, He 'created man in his own image, after his own likeness.' And what was the end of his creation? It was one, and no other—that he might know, and love, and enjoy, and serve his great Creator to all eternity. . . .
>
> Remember! You were born for nothing else. You live for nothing else. Your life is continued to you upon earth, for no other purpose than this, that you may know, love, and serve God on earth, and enjoy him to all eternity. Consider! You were not created to please your senses, to gratify your imagination, to gain money, or the praise of men; to seek happiness in any created good, in anything

under the sun. All this is 'walking in a vain shadow'; it is leading a restless, miserable life, in order to a miserable eternity. On the contrary, you were created for this, and for no other purpose, by seeking and finding happiness in God on earth, to secure the glory of God in heaven.[1]

In yet another sermon, Wesley develops his teaching concerning the ultimate end of human life as follows:

The one perfect Good shall be your one ultimate end. One thing shall ye desire for its own sake,—the fruition of Him that is All in all. One happiness shall ye propose to your souls, even an union with Him that made them; the having 'fellowship with the Father and the Son'; the being joined to the Lord in one Spirit. One design you are to pursue to the end of time,—the enjoyment of God in time and in eternity. Desire other things, so far as they tend to this. Love the creature, as it leads to the Creator. But in every step you take, be this the glorious point that terminates your view. Let every affection, and thought, and word, and work, be subordinate to this. Whatever ye desire or fear, whatever ye seek or shun, whatever ye think, speak or do, be it in order to your happiness in God, the sole End, as well as Source, of your being.
Have no end, no ultimate end, but God.[2]

Clearly, these teachings can be rightly understood only in their larger context in Wesley's witness and theology. But that they are in every sense characteristic teachings, which he constantly expresses or implies, will be clear at once to anyone acquainted with his writings. Moreover, since among the other writings in which they are set forth are some that have enjoyed the status of doctrinal standards in Methodist churches, it is just as clear that the answer they give to our question is a representative Free-Church answer. The issue before us here, however, is the *systematic* theological issue of whether this old answer is still adequate; and on this issue my position is that one can reasonably conclude that it is not—indeed, that it is neither appropriate nor understandable, given what these general criteria require in our special situation today.

Consider, first, the present requirements of understandability. It is widely agreed by contemporary theologians that these requirements are decisively shaped by certain assumptions concerning meaning and truth that are typically made in the present human situation. That situation, in the words of J. H. Oldham, is 'determined and dominated by two main influences. The first is the rise of modern science and the growth of technology. The other is the resolve of man to use his increasing knowledge and technical skill to shape his environment, his society, and himself and to control his own destiny'.[3] Given this kind of historical situation, the standards of what makes sense and can be accepted as true are set by assumptions concerning the ultimate reality and significance of the present world in which we live and the responsibility that each of us bears for so changing our societies and cultures that all our possibilities as creatures may be fully realized.

But if these assumptions are not only made but are also in keeping with the standards of meaning and truth implicit in human existence, then Wesley's answer to the question of the meaning of human life can hardly be understandable. On the contrary, in its assertions that we are sent into the world for no other purpose than to prepare for eternity and that the one thing we shall desire for its own sake is our individual enjoyment of God, it expresses the kind of otherworldliness and individualism that persons in our situation today are so far from accepting as true as barely even to find intelligible. Nor is the primary reason for this the more strictly theoretical objections that can obviously be made to the whole idea of another world and of our continued subjective existence beyond death. By far the more serious objection to any such assertions is that, in focusing our attention on our eventual enjoyment of good in eternity, they divert us from our present responsibility for the realization of good in time, by providing at least a negative sanction for the social and cultural *status quo*.

Of course, the fact, if it be a fact, that Wesley's answer fails to meet the requirements of understandability need not mean that it likewise fails to meet the requirements of appropriateness. There remains the possibility that, although the otherworldliness and individualism of his answer can no longer be assessed as meaningful and true, his are nevertheless the only terms in which the Christian understanding of human existence can be expressed so as to be the same as that expressed in the normative Christian witness. In that event, obviously, the conclusion one would have to draw is not only that this old answer is no longer adequate but that the same must be true of any new answer that is appropriately Christian. But if I am right, there is no reason to draw so drastic a conclusion, since the appropriateness of Wesley's answer today is just as questionable as its understandability.

A NEW UNDERSTANDING OF GOD

The main reason for questioning its appropriateness is that it by no means teaches consistently that God himself is the sole ultimate end of human life. Although Wesley expressly asserts that it is God who is 'the sole End, as well as Source', of our being and, accordingly, lays down the imperative, 'Have no end, no ultimate end, but God', he also asserts several times over that our ultimate end is our own enjoyment or fruition of God, or our own happiness in him. But this, clearly, is to give two inconsistent answers to the question of the ultimate end of human life. For if that end is our own enjoyment or happiness, even our enjoyment of God or our happiness in him, then God himself is not the final end of our being but at best the means to its realization. On the other hand, if the sole ultimate end of our life really is God himself, then everything else, even our enjoyment of God or our happiness in him, is at best a means to that one ultimate end.

To be sure, no one could deny that there is ample precedent in traditional Christian witness and theology for this inconsistency in Wesley's teaching. As a matter of fact, the same inconsistency might appear to be so prominent in the Christian tradition as to count rather for than against the appropriateness of Wesley's answer. But if we distinguish, as we can and must, between the Christian understanding of human existence, on the one hand, and the terms in which that understanding has traditionally been expressed, on the other, we may well ask whether such inconsistency in teaching that God alone is our ultimate end has not been due precisely to the terms of the witness. After all, these terms have been provided, for the most part, either by a mythical representation of human fulfilment as continued enjoyment of God beyond death (whether through resurrection of the body or through immortality of the soul) or by a metaphysical interpretation of divine perfection as strict immutability, from which it follows that, since neither man or any other creature could make even the least difference to God, he could not be consistently conceived as their ultimate end.

In other words, one could fully explain the inconsistency of the Christian tradition even if one were to argue, as I would, that it is as essential to Christian witness and theology to maintain that God himself is the only final end of all things as to hold that he himself is their only primal source. Even so, to argue that convincingly, one would have to show that the only appropriate expression of the apostolic witness contained in the New Testament, which alone is normative Christian witness, requires just that insistence that God himself is our only ultimate end which is so marked a characteristic of the New Testament writings themselves—as, for example, when Paul teaches that for us as Christians, 'there is one God, the Father, from whom are all things and for whom we exist' and that, whatever we do, it is 'to the glory of God' that it is all to be done (1 Cor. 8:6, 10:31).

If this can be shown, as I believe it can, Wesley's answer is evidently doubly inadequate, being no more appropriate than it is understandable. Precisely in order to meet the present requirements of appropriateness one must break decisively with the whole long tradition of which his answer is an expression and consistently conceive the objective God himself, rather than our subjective enjoyment of him, as the only ultimate end of our life. Of course, to do this, one must depend on terms other than those of the main theological tradition. For if God himself is the ultimate end of our life, then he must be conceived and symbolized not only as the one integral *cause* of all things but also, and just as importantly, as their one integral *effect*. But such terms are clearly available to us in the revisionary metaphysics of our own time, and we are without excuse if we continue to think and speak in ways that imply that the ultimate end of human life were something other than God himself and his glory.

Finally, whatever doubts may remain about the meaning and truth of any Christian answer to the question of life's meaning, an answer cast in these revisionary terms at least overcomes the more serious objection to the understandability of Wesley's answer to the question. For if the God who is himself the ultimate end of our life is the One to whom no creature can fail to make a difference and whose greatest glory consists in enjoying the fullest realization of each creature's possibilities, then to focus attention on *his* everlasting enjoyment of all good is in no way to divert us from our own responsibility here and now for the maximal realization of good. On the contrary, it is to witness that the deeper meaning of all our realization of good, whether the emancipation realized only by social and cultural change or the salvation realized only by individual faith working through love, is nothing less than the greater glory of God.

If we are to find a new answer to the old question that will be adequate for our time, it is along these lines that we will have to seek it.

Notes

1. Thomas Jackson (ed.), *The Works of the Rev. John Wesley, A.M.* (London, [3]1829–31), vol. 7, pp. 229–30.

2. Edward H. Sugden (ed.), *Wesley's Standard Sermons* (London, 1921), vol. 1, pp. 273–74.

3. *Life Is Commitment* (London, 1953), p. 14.

PART III

Suggestions for a New Answer

Jan Dobraczyński

A European Answer

WHY has God called us to be Christians? I belong to a generation which opened its eyes to the world in a state of unfreedom entered into by my people when at the end of the eighteenth century the Polish state was torn into fragments by neighbouring countries. I belong to a generation which in 1918 greeted the long-desired independence and reconstruction of the national presence only to be compelled, after twenty years of freedom, to witness the re-subjection of the reborn fatherland to aggression and several years of suffering under enemy occupation.

I also belong to a generation which experienced a great religious renewal in the nineteen-thirties. In Poland, a country that is Catholic by tradition but also one that was known all over the world for its religious tolerance, young people underwent a revival of religious feeling on the eve of the second World War, at a time when in many European countries the emphasis was on nationalistic sentiments and tendencies. To the ideology of the racist state Poland opposed its ideal of a 'Christian state', which was not perhaps very practical and perhaps even naive, but nevertheless quite sincere.

We were thrown into armed conflict. Our ideal did not guarantee us victory. Those who acknowledged that ideal lost their lives in the September campaign of 1939, in the resistance movement, in the partisan war, in the Warsaw uprising of 1944, and in prisons and concentration camps. When victory finally arrived, it was not the triumph of an idea in which people had believed, for another world view arrived with it.

We who had experienced all these things were faced with disturbing questions. Is Christianity incapable of triumphing in such circumstances? Is it a world view which offers its followers no more than eternal life and ascribes them no rôle here on earth? Are we Christians perhaps only on earth in order to save our souls through defeat and death?

For us the post-war years were a period of fundamental and often harsh rethinking. In order to think of the future, we had to escape our feeling of disillusionment, and once again analyze the ideals of the nineteen-thirties.

During the war we were often extremely shocked by the inscription *Gott mit uns* (God with us) on the belt buckles of German soldiers. What annoys us in others is often an indication of our own weak points. In those years of constant examination of conscience we often became aware of how easy it is to foist our own wishes onto the idea we believe in. When we fight for things which we look on as divine, all too often we tend to identify them with our own efforts and our own interests. We tend to shape God according to our own human norms.

Jesus said 'Whoever is not against you is for you' and continued: 'Whoever is not with me is against me'. In the latter instance he was addressing the Pharisees when they objected that he drove out demons through the power of Beelzebub. In the light of an accusation of that kind the differentiation had to be very exact. In the first case however Jesus was speaking to his disciples, to future missionaries, and therefore to those who were to continue his work. His words are to be understood as stating that the disciples must not forget that they had no monopoly of God. God came to us all and it is his will that those ways too must be attended to on which searchers are journeying for whom the normal road is momentarily blocked.

In the history of Poland this problem already occurred in the fifteenth century. At the Council of Constance, the Cracow Canon Pawel Wlodkowic from Brudzevo engaged in public debate with representatives of the German Order of Knights on the conversion of the Prussians 'with fire and sword'. He said: 'We are not permitted to force unbelievers to assume the Christian faith with weapons in our hands or by some other show of force, because we would then be doing an injustice to our neighbours. Furthermore we cannot do such a thing, for we are never allowed to do evil that good may come of it . . . No one is to be forced to adopt the faith . . . Whoever uses such force serves his own ends and not the ends of God'.

Of course things are somewhat different today. The time of conversion with fire and sword is past, and also the period of missions working in close conjunction with colonialism is at an end. But the problem is no different. We Christians feel responsible for the world. We do not live in this world just in order to save our souls. In the Middle Ages the opinion was widely heard that whoever possesses the truth is entitled to impose it on others. Now we want to convince others of our truth. That is our duty.

The modern world shows no genuine interest in things divine, even though there is repeated evidence of a longing for spiritual values. It has no time for the things of God. It is too strongly engaged by the rate at which life is lived, by astonishing discoveries, by the exploration of the universe, by the search for comfort and entertainment, and too fascinated by the illusion of unbridled sex. This world, symbolized by television with its unceasing chatter, its excess of useless information, its hodge-podge of sensationalism, its self-exaltation through the creation of a number of stars, deprives man of the last fragment of time left to him for meditation.

There is only one world and there is no escaping it. We must recall Teilhard de Chardin's vision of the ultimate synthesis: the totalization of humanity concentrated by a process of organic pressure. The process of totalization seems to suit the conception of Teilhard as a fanatic visionary and mystic.

This synthesis, though it accords with Teilhard's thought, contains both risk and opportunity. The advent of totalization does not have to lead automatically to a supra-hominization. 'Life is', as Teilhard says, 'less certain than death' *(La Place de l'Homme dans la Nature)*.

The major ideologies of our time are helpless in the face of the negative effects of the totalization of the world. They were useful in the era of striving for totalization, when they supported its tendency and took advantage of the positive effects of the process; but as soon as change faces them with a situation that seems liable to lead to catastrophe, they lose all potency.

Only Christianity, I am quite convinced, sees the danger and at the same time the great opportunity of this aspect of synthesis. Trustworthy and humble (which was its weakness at a time when the advancing process of concentration brought great riches, developed technology, drew the masses along with it, and ensured the victory), thanks to the same qualities, it now has the power that allows it to find a way out of an apparently hopeless situation. Of course that escape route does not appear of itself. In order to find it we have to trust and to act. It is the task of Christians on this earth to work with all those who are looking for a way which leads to a further phase of human development.

It was fortunate, a really prophetic stroke, that the Augustinian model of the *Civitas Dei* lost its historical value and disappeared, and that Christians were forced to enter the ocean of humanity. Without the will to impose the truth and without their protective walls they advanced into the maelstrom of a world of reputation and strength. They have nothing but their own lives with which to convince the world of the truth.

Experience shows us that intellectual dialogue is incapable of overcoming contradictions when unaccompanied by that inner dialogue a man conducts with himself. This dialogue depends on continuous confrontation of our own thoughts and experiences with the truth that we acknowledge. The dialogue might be summarized as follows: Being a Christian means letting Christ live in us. To want to represent Christianity without experiencing it is an obvious mistake. The position of the weaker partner has to be comprehended in a dialogue conducted with others. In our contacts with those who stand for another world view, we have frequently seen that our position is only influential if we can add living testimony to our verbal arguments.

Christianity today is a Christianity with a missionary impulse. We might paraphrase slightly Péguy's words, 'The crusades are coming to us' by saying that 'the missions are coming to us'. The present mission means however announcing the Gospel by sharing in the life of the world: by sharing in its fate, and thus serving the world as Mother Teresa of Calcutta has served it.

Service of mankind does not only mean discovering extremely tragic situations at the other end of the world. The loneliness which men in general experience in the world today also means that we do not have to look far for an area for our activity.

Jan Salamucha, the Polish philosopher and logician, who died in the Warsaw rising, defined Catholicism as an 'open dogmatic system' that must be continually extended.

That process of extension seems nowadays to consist in our entry as Christians wholly and completely into the life of the world, so that we make our contribution to the humanization of the process of ultimate concentration: so that the evolution of mankind can reach Point Omega on its way.

Translated by John Griffiths

John Garvey

A North American Answer

THE QUESTION 'Why am I on this earth' was extended by Pascal: 'When I consider the short duration of my life, swallowed up in the eternity before and after, the little space which I fill, and even can see, engulfed in the infinite immensity of spaces of which I am ignorant, and which know me not, I am frightened, and astonished at being here rather than there; for there is no reason why here rather than there, why now rather than then. Who has put me here? By whose order and direction have this time and place been allotted to me?' (*Pensées*, fragment 205)

It is this odd, *particular* nature of our being here which haunts us, and it is this aspect of our questioning which the old catechetical answer was least able to address. The Christian may see, because of faith, 'by whose order and direction have this time and place been allotted', but the question which Christianity is being asked, especially in America and the Western world as a whole, is *what difference being a Christian makes*. Answering this will involve us in a self-examination which is less comfortable than any we have had to undertake in recent Christian history, in large part because of the complicity of Christians in creating a society which is based on greed and waste, and which produces despair. It is not an exaggeration to say that our society is based on waste and greed; it is a fact that our economy would collapse if people did not spend most of their energy acquiring what they do not need, and pursuing a sense of self which the Gospel tells us we must lose, in order to begin to be alive.

Christians have not co-operated in the creation of such a society wickedly or cynically; we have simply been too uncritical of its values. Wherever Christians have adopted the values of the dominant culture uncritically they have been weak witnesses to the Gospel. The

Churches tend too often to stress a limited, excessively personalistic ethic, combined with church attendance and sacramental participation; this, they say in practice, is what the Gospel is about—not a transformed humanity, merely a slightly different one, one which behaves better. This not only contradicts the radical claims of the Gospel; it avoids confronting the deepest reasons we have been given for rejoicing.

In his book *To Jerusalem and Back* the American novelist Saul Bellow mentions the difference between the consciousness of Soviet dissidents, as revealed in their writing, and the consciousness which prevails in the West. The dissidents have a quality of constant alertness, where the West drifts in and out of sleep, almost as if there were things we choose not to know. The same clarity can, I think, be detected in the church which suffers around the world—in South Korea, the Philippines, Brazil, South Africa, Uganda, as well as the Soviet bloc. There is among these Christians an alertness, a willingness to drop everything for the sake of the Gospel—including life, if that is required. Next to this courageous and uncluttered Christianity the Churches of the industrialized West look pale and decadent. We must turn to these Churches to begin to understand our vocation, and find teachers who can help us.

There is a Buddhist story which says that when Gautama Buddha was asked 'Who are you? Are you a God? A demon? A sage?' he answered 'I am awake'. The consciousness which all religion calls for has nothing to do with belonging to an organization, or even with the more involving allegiance demanded by political ideologies. It involves a quality of alertness, attention, awareness within a context which is at once critical of the information it receives, and absolutely open to the information which other ways of living and believing make available to us. When Christianity offers a view of reality which contradicts the reality experienced by most people on earth, or which offers oversimplified explanations of that reality, it does not serve the human beings for whom Jesus died, and for whose liberation he rose.

The context which Professor Küng sets for asking the old catechetical question, and attempting a modern answer, rightly demands an end to the convenient separations between the divine and the human, the religious and the secular, the here and the hereafter, which conservative Christians and their anti-religious opponents both cherish. But once these separations have been seen through, new contradictions between Christianity and the *Zeitgeist* appear, and they show themselves in the dialogue between Christianity and other attempts— religious as well as non-religious—at answering the question, 'Why am I here?' Professor Küng points out how well the focus of Hinduism and

Buddhism shows up the self-seeking shallowness of Western individualism. The ancient religious answers take on a fresh significance in the most violent century in human history, a time which certainly confirms the darkest message of any religion, and challenges Christianity more deeply than any, given the fact that the skies over Auschwitz were silent. Of course there is no easy reconciliation between intense human suffering and the doctrine of an all-powerful, infinitely loving God; but never has the belief been so challenged. We are used to believing (and it is a 'being used to', a habit more than a real conviction) that Jesus' messianic rôle revealed the inadequacy of previous Jewish definitions of the Messiah, which we have much too confidently dismissed as 'worldly'. Trying to overcome simple distinctions between the human and the divine, the earthly and the heavenly, we will find ourselves confronted with Christianity's Jewish heritage, which never made those distinctions. The inadequacy of the ordinary Christian definition of Jesus as the Messiah may reveal itself and suggest new approaches. In the face of the fact that the world is so obviously unredeemed, how do we proclaim the reality of redemption? To tell a person that he is free, and ignore the bars which enclose him; to tell a hungry man that he has been fed, but the bread was merely metaphorical; to ignore the fact that the world is apparently in thrall to *something* that does not love human beings; to do any of these things is obscene, but unfortunately this is a style which characterizes the kind of Christianity which dominates the West. One central task of a renewed Christian proclamation must be an understanding of a Christian's rôle in messianic liberation.

The importance of making the radical self-examination asked for here is particularly crucial for Christians whose outlook is so pervaded by the noise, clutter, and glut of American, Western European, and Japanese culture, and here a restoration of the contemplative spirit is called for. We are bored, and look constantly for things to distract ourselves with. Our desire always to be interested is feverish, a constant itch. We want to do everything but what we most need to do: sit quietly and face the uncomfortable words of the Gospel and the bothersome life at its centre.

We must, finally, realize that for most of the world Christianity is far from being a self-evident good. As long as an acceptable (and even respectable) Christianity can co-exist with self-interest, waste, individualism, the worship of political or nationalistic solutions to our problems, and a fear of the demands of those who suffer, the church as an institution may thrive. But the message of the Gospel will move down the scale from good news, to decent news, to news, to one idea among many, to a banal and perhaps pretty picture of a world much too simple and cozy to be true. And when honest seekers after truth turn to agnosticism, which seems at least true to the facts, or to one of the eastern religions, which are able at least to face the suffering at the heart of life, we may be able to say with some justice that they are somewhat naive to have made such a choice. But we will not be able to say so confidently that they were quite wrong to reject the Churches in their search for an answer to the question posed by the catechism.

Ernesto Cardenal

A Latin American Answer:
On Lake Nicaragua

Dark black sky with all its stars.
Mid-lake in an old boat,
the *Maria Danelia*.
I'm looking up at them
as I lie in the stern on some sacks of rice.
I've just been interrogated by the Military Court
and I think of the enormous worlds above us,
a single galaxy
(if Earth was like a grain of rice
the galaxy would be like Jupiter's orbit).
And I think of Comrade 'Modesto' in the mountain,
of peasant birth, his name unknown.
They are fighting to accomplish our destiny in the galaxy.
And the peasants hung by their wrists,
dragged out of eggs.
A child of eight had its throat cut, say the Capuchins.
Prisoners piled in public lavatories,
on top of each other, women, children, the old.
And these bright worlds,
the society of the stars
turning about us.
The Kingdom of Heaven irradiating light years
('. . . which was prepared for you from the foundation of the world'),
since the primordial gas
emerged from the black, cold inter-stellar spaces

and concentrated
and became warmer and brighter.
Perhaps we'll return to the inter-stellar spaces?
And may not life
be as characteristic of the universe
as light?
How far in space-time!
But we do not see all the light. In the rainbow
beyond the violet lies the invisible ultra-violet,
and there is another ultra beyond the ultra-violet,
the zone of love.
From the *Maria Danelia* and dark Nicaraguan water
I see the universe of light, the curve
of light. Like night-flying over New York.
Or rather:
the stars of the galaxy grasped in a handful
like a troupe of dancers round a fire
and Pythagoras heard the rattles.
The centre of the Milky Way is not a great star
but a concentration of stars
(yonder by the constellation of Sagittarius).
What I see are about 1000 worlds,
astronomers can see nearly a billion:
'love evolution'.
In Cuba schools, hospitals, nurseries
are sprouting like mushrooms after rain.
Gravity is merely the curving of the universe,
its yearning for union.
We have a common centre and it is before us.
Many arrested, others in hiding.
They bomb peasants from helicopters.
To give life is to surrender to the future.
To be one body with a single mind,
all together, wanting the same.
The president of the Court said:
'Do you realize they fight for the poor?
Answer yes or no'.
To change into something greater than one.
All is movement: galaxy, solar system, planet
together with *Maria Danelia,* the Lorios' old boat
all sailing through space-time.
'I believe they fight for the poor'.
I was called to the Court

and I did your will.
I look up at the stars and say:
I have kept your commandments.
In our small corner, the planetary revolution,
mankind without classes,
the reason
the planet goes round the sun.
Unification
of the universe!
And the 'outer-darkness':
the inter-stellar spaces?
All is movement.
Your will be done,
on this planet as it is in the galaxies.

Translated by Dinah Livingstone

John Mbiti

An African Answer

THIS QUESTION has never engaged my thoughts seriously. I would not even raise it in the context of my traditional African setting. I have come across it only in the western Christian setting. Therefore I answer it only as someone else's question. In an African setting it would be considered very rude or curse-worthy, for a person to ask his or her parents: 'Why did you bear me?' In the same attitude of mind, a similar question would not be posed about God creating someone. In the hope that I do not offend against this traditional etiquette, I venture to make some comments in answer to the question: 'Why did God make me?'

In African mythology we get some glimpses of an answer to this problem. The Abaluyia (of Kenya) tell that God created man so that the sun would have someone for whom to shine. The Lugbara (of Uganda) hold that God created man in order to 'people' the earth just as he had 'peopled' the sky. The Shilluk (of the Sudan) narrate that God created man out of clay, 'then he gave man legs with which to walk and run; hands with which to plant grain; eyes with which to see that grain and a mouth with which to eat it. Afterwards God gave him the tongue with which to sing and talk; and finally ears, so that he may enjoy the sound of music, of dance and of the talk of great men. Then God sent man out, a complete man'.

In African religion, many references are made to God as Father (or Mother) of man. This analogy has to be seen against the African social background in which it is considered absolutely necessary that everyone should bear children. A person is not 'complete', 'perfect', 'whole', without bearing children. In this case, therefore, the creation of man by God is an expression of His perfectness, wholeness, completeness. Thus, God makes or creates man, not for what man would do or be, but because of God's own nature of wholeness.

There follows, from this parent-child relationship between God and man, that man regards God as father, mother, provider, giver of good things, protector, saviour from danger and trouble, and so on. In many prayers, Africans address God in this spirit of parental relationship. For example, in time of starvation the Konde (of Tanzania) invoke God thus: 'Thou art our Father and we are thy children. Thou hast created us'.

The question of the parents-children relationship is not difficult to accommodate within one's social and conceptual framework. What is difficult, and what people seem to ask is: having been made by God, why do I suffer? why am I sick? why am I hungry when others have enough to eat? why do I lose my close relative through death? why has the drought hit us this season? why have the locusts visited and devastated our fields? why does my child fail his examinations while others pass them? The agonizing search comes out clearly in a traditional prayer from Burundi-Rwanda: 'Imana (God), why are you punishing me? Why have you not made me like other people? Couldn't you even give me one little child, Yo-o-o! I am dying in anguish . . . O Imana, you have deserted me!'

In African attitudes, nature is 'sacred' and man has a priestly relationship with it. He is the religious conscience of the universe, looked at from the centrality of man. People have used, and largely continue to use, almost everything within their reach to make offerings and sacrifices to God and other spiritual realities. Man engages in a process of the sacralization of nature; and man treats nature with sacral respect. This is the ideal, and there is much abuse directed against nature as well. One prayer from the Didinga people (of the Sudan) illustrates this very clearly. It is used at the sowing season, by the chief ritual leader of the people: 'O Earth, wherever it be my people dig, be kindly to them. Be fertile when they give the little seeds to your keeping. Let your generous warmth nourish them and your abundant moisture germinate them . . . O trees of forest and glade, fall easily under the axe. Be gentle to my people. Let no harm come to them. Break no limb in your anger. Crush no one in your displeasure . . . Submit yourselves freely to my people, as this tree has submitted itself to me . . . O rivers and streams, where the woodman has laid bare the earth, where he has hewn away the little bushes and torn out encumbering grass, there let your waters overflow . . . When the rains swell your banks, spread out your waters and lay your rich treasures on our gardens' (J. S. Mbiti, *The Prayers of African Religion,* London, 1975, pp. 69 f.).

Man has to harmonize nature with his priestly function. Without man, nature (the earth) would be rough, rigid, and wild. Without man, the earth would be full of thorns and weeds. This African concept comes close to the Genesis statement that 'the Lord God took the man and put him in the garden of Eden to till it and keep it' (Genesis 2:15). In this respect, man is the direct link between God and the earth, shouldering a pastoral responsibility over the earth with all that is in it. It is through man that the earth relates to God in a unique way.

The fact that man is linked with God, through creation, would make one feel that we are on the earth as an expression of God's own being. Yet when we see the 'inconsistencies' of life—such as suffering, injustice, and death—then the question of why God made man becomes very acute. While in the middle of writing this article, news reached me that a close cousin of mine had just lost her husband through sudden death. She is now a young widow, with eight small children. One asks not why God has made, but why God has taken away this young man, leaving such young children without a father. This and similar cases can be duplicated the world over.

Man is made to partake of the mystery of life and death. Life flares for a short while, for individual persons, then comes the transformation through the gate of death. God makes man in order to remake him through this painful transformation process. The insights from African religion, and the basis of our Christian faith, lead us to reject the notion that death can have the final say over life. God creates the individual out of non-existence and endows him with a life which cannot be again reduced to non-existence. Man is made to demonstrate, and to become conscious of the fact of life over non-life (death). It cannot be that man is made for death. Man must be made for life and life in its entire wholeness. Since God is life in its entirety and wholeness, he created man as an intelligent extension of that wholeness of being. Yet we see this human share of God's wholeness riddled by many wounds and marked by many scars from both nature and man himself. But it is precisely at this point that the mystery of the cross-and-resurrection of our Lord brings us hope that somehow in the course of time those scars will be removed, and the absolute wholeness of man will be restored or mediated in and through Him who shared in being made like us, in living, in dying and uniquely in rising again. And this wholeness must also be corporate—man made whole within the cosmos which also is made whole. But one can say this and anticipate it only in faith, since there could be other possibilities that await mankind and the cosmos, hidden in the wisdom of God. While keeping hold of this eschatological hope, we do not ask why God made man—a question which only God can answer, if it must be asked—, but rather, we are overwhelmed by the wonder of it all, that God has made man and man is aware of Him as his Creator = Father-Mother.

Julia Ching

An Asian Answer

TO ASK this question of an intellectual of the East Asian (namely, Chinese) cultural heritage, is to urge first an examination of various traditional and modern Chinese—non-Christian—answers. I refer here to four in particular: the Confucian, Taoist, Buddhist and Maoist.

THE CHINESE NON-CHRISTIAN ANSWERS

The 'moralist' answer: the Confucian sees human life in terms of striving for ethical perfection, with sagehood as an earthly goal to be achieved. Such perfection is to be acquired especially through social virtues, governing one's relationship within the family (as parent or child, husband or wife, elder or younger brother) as well as without (as ruler or subject, and as friends). It is not yet a completely 'outmoded' answer, since Confucian ethics remains the warp and woof of much of East Asian life, and had to be 'combatted' in the People's Republic of China even after twenty-five years of Communist rule.

The 'naturalist' answer: the Taoist sees human life in terms of its harmony with nature, urging for simplicity, and—in the case of Chuang-tzu and his spiritual heirs—avoidance of social involvements. The Taoist is usually an individualist, sometimes a hermit. He prefers nature to culture, aesthetic beauty to ethical distinctions.

The 'religious-mystical' answer: the Chinese Buddhist is usually of the Mahayana persuasion, desiring to help bring about universal, even cosmic salvation rather than concentrating merely upon saving himself. In the case of the Pure Land follower, this zeal is accompanied by an explicit faith in the name of the Buddha. In the case of the Ch'an (Zen) initiate, the focus is on personal enlightenment and mystical self-transformation. The ideal is the Bodhisattva, who foregoes his own Nirvana to save others.

The 'political' answer: the Chinese Marxist (Maoist) sees his life-task as that of 'serving the People', particularly the People of China, but in a revolutionary fellowship with all 'real' Marxists in the world—especially the Third World. The emphasis is upon the construction of an ideal socialist society, according to the teachings of the deceased Chairman Mao.

A comparison of these four answers shows quickly a closer relationship between the Taoist and Buddhist positions on the one hand, and the Confucian and Maoist positions on the other—which explains the ground for rivalry between Confucianism and Maoism in today's China, as well as the gradual historical amalgamation of Taoism and Buddhism, each with its eremitical or manoastic tradition. Except for the extreme individualist, the social dimension is present in most Chinese answers, whether actually or intentionally, with the state and society preferred today over the family.

Except for the Pure Land Buddhist, however, there is little attention to God and faith. This does not necessarily exclude a belief in God. But this emphasizes an implicit sense of self-confidence with regard to the task of self-perfection, be that carried out by a Confucian gentleman, a Taoist or Ch'an (Zen) contemplative, or a Maoist patriot or revolutionary. The Chinese attitude is clearly world-affirming, even for the Mahayana Buddhist or the nature-loving Taoist.

Speaking historically, many Christian missionaries recognized the beauty of the Chinese ideals of self-perfection. In his late sixteenth-century catechism (*The True Idea of God*), Matteo Ricci attempted to convert a hypothetical Chinese friend to the directing of his effort of self-perfection as a Confucian to a motivation of love of the Christian God. The Chinese pointed out the inherent difficulty of such a leap, since the invitation to faith rests entirely upon the testimony of the missionary himself, as messenger of the invisible God, whose own faith, in turn, was based on the words of others who never saw God. For a stranger to the Christian tradition, this kind of near-infinite regression can become almost insurmountable.

THE CHINESE CHRISTIAN ANSWER

For the Chinese today who is already Christian, faith has become part of his personal heritage, that which he shares with a minority of his compatriots. He remains conscious of his share in a larger cultural patrimony, which includes the traditional attitudes towards life and the world, whether Confucian, Taoist or Buddhist. He is also conscious of the recent political history which has made China a Communist country—a history provoked in large part by Western imperialism, political and cultural, to which the missionary movement, at least since the nineteenth century, also belonged. He has perhaps been accused of a lack of patriotism, since Christianity signifies to many patriots an alien loyalty in the same way that Buddhism or even Confucianism signifies to a Maoist a 'feudal' mentality. The modern Chinese Christian knows therefore the conflicts of the earlier catechumen or convert, as well as newer ones.

Why is he or she in this world? The answer must be a personal one, a very independent one, born of inner conflicts and outer confrontations.

The Chinese Christian is an 'individual', who must continually assert his Christianity in spite of the culturally and politcally alienating effects of this assertion. To remain Christian, his faith must become the core of his life. He is in this world to believe, and to live according to his beliefs, This is a voluntarist answer, but characteristic of those who have accepted Christianity prinicpally on the testimony of others, rather than also as part of their own cultural and social heritage.

A Chinese Christian is part of a 'community', whether the Chinese exodus, or the Communist society. He remains conscious of his social responsibilities—an integral part of his traditional heritage, which has received a new political direction from Maoism. A Chinese Christian feels a special responsibility toward his country and his compatriots, in the construction of a socialist society, if he continues to live in China, or, toward the culture he represents, as is frequently the experience of overseas Chinese.

The contemporary Chinese Christian world-view is therefore an intensely personal combination of traditional cultural and modern political answers. It is also a dialectical synthesis of conflicting loyalites which makes the call to self-transcendence all the more challenging and perhaps disconcerting. A Chinese Christian may sense himself a kind of tragic hero. He has a real commitment in faith to the Christian cause. But he also recognizes the continual pull of this commitment, setting him apart from his fellow compatriots, making his situation unique, and rendering his personal moral burden heavier.

THE CHRISTIAN CONTRIBUTION

The traditional Christian answer used to be: we are in this world to serve God and to save our souls. To the world-affirming Chinese, this appeared too spiritualistic and other-worldly, giving the invisible God the central role in human life, and representing the invisible soul as wayward and in need of salvation. Its claims are at once too much and not enough: too much, because of the knowledge of God, and not enough, because of the neglect of the positive values of this life.

The modern Christian answers emphasize happiness in this world as well as the next (Dutch catechism), the social dimension of life and our earthly-historical task (Hans Küng). In becoming so world-affirming, it has converged with the traditional Chinese, especially Confucian answer.

The specific, Christian contribution lies in the example of Jesus Christ, an integral part of both traditional and modern Christian answers to the meaning of life. For both the Western European and the East Asian believer, he is a source of trust and inspiration. The traditional Chinese answers have not coped with the problem of suffering, with the exception of Buddhism, which pointed a way to deliverance from suffering. The example of the suffering Jesus was a stumbling block for many would-be believers but also a source of strength for those who have accepted him.

THE CHINESE CONTRIBUTION TO THE CHRISTIAN WORLD VIEW

The Chinese experience of Christianity can serve a *negative* function in promoting Christian awareness of past misdeeds, of missionary mistakes based primarily on religious and dogmatic triumphalism. Christianity has indeed added to the cross of the Chinese, particularly of the believer. As such, this experience calls for a greater and humbler understanding of China, and indeed of the non-Christian world as a whole.

But the Chinese Christian presence can also make a *positive* contribution to the Christian world view itself. It does so by reconfirming the modern affirmation of this life and this world, and the social responsibility of the Christian. It can do more by bringing to Christianity a broader perspective of the human self, of man as part of a larger whole, whether familial, social, or cosmic. Hence it can help to correct the traditional, individualistic emphasis on 'personal' salvation, and to strengthen the modern, 'communal' emphasis of Christian fellowship and ecumenical unity,—and that, in a secular world roughly divided between the individualistic, free-enterprise systems of the Christian and post-Christian West, and the collectivistic, Communist societies of the post-Christian and non-Christian East.

The Chinese Christian presence has always been that of a minority, of a *diaspora* living amid a non-believing environment. As such, it may have something special to say to the shrinking Christian community as a whole, itself become a *diaspora* living in a secularized world, whether capitalist or Communist.

Why are we in this world? Among other things, it is to learn from one another, so as to be able to serve God better in one another, in this world, and to be happy, with him and with one another—both in this world and the next.

PART IV

Assessment and Synthesis

Jürgen Moltmann

God's Kingdom as the Meaning of Life and of the World

IT WOULD be arrogant to attempt a 'synthesis' of the riches contained in these contributions which come from different Christian traditions and different socio-cultural situations. Yet, one has to be clear about what this ecumenical study has produced in order to have some perspective for a common future. This 'common future' should be understood as embracing both the future of a common public justification of the faith and the future of a world for which all men are responsible in common. The old passage of the catechism contains both: questions conditioned by man's situation and responsible belief. I shall therefore first sum up the critique and assessment of the question and answer contained in the catechism as presented in this issue, and in both cases from the point of view of ecumenism, apologetics and theology.

CRITIQUE OF THE QUESTION

The astonishing result of the inquiry is the fact that this catechism question has been so wide-spread since the sixteenth century together with its fundamental importance for the justification of the Christian faith. Here the Catholic, Orthodox, Reformed and Free Church (Methodist) traditions are at one even in the formulation, and all start with this question. The only diversion is the Lutheran tradition which starts with the divine law in which man's existence is contained. But the question about the meaning of being a Christian at the beginning of the Lutheran catechism can in any case be traced to the end of that century. The German Reformed tradition also begins in this way

(*Heidelberger Katechismus,* 1563). These divergences themselves already show a certain criticism of the theological starting-point which should be dealt with in the ecumenical dialogue.

The question occurs in various forms: Why has God created me? Why are we on this earth? What is the main end of man's life? The contributions are in general agreement that this question refers to the meaning of life. Since life does not evidently bear its meaning only in itself, conscious life has to look for its meaning in order to accept and mould itself on the basis of the answer. The old ways of formulating this question about the meaning of life have, however, been criticised: Can this question about the meaning be expressed in the form of questions about the cause and end of life? In the age of our modern end-means-rationalization this is impossible (Charlesworth). When human life is only justified through lists of aims and utilitarian values, inhumanity will dominate. At this point the Lutheran suspicion (Persson) seems to be confirmed that the metaphysical formulation of the catechism question reduces life to a 'means towards an end' and subjects it to the cramping justification through works. Even a life without aim and useless is still a meaningful life in God's eyes. Life on earth cannot be reduced to a mere 'means towards an end' in terms of faith and hope, it must also be accepted and loved as an 'end-in-itself'.

This also concerns the Creator of man. Questions about the why and the wherefore are inclined to by-pass God's free good will which lies at the root of his creating, presides over his creation and with which this creation should be in harmony. Questions about why and wherefore seem to equate 'meaningful' with 'necessary' in order to wipe out the impression we have of the fortuitousness of our existence. But should we not say about creation as a whole as about our own existence: meaningful, yet not necessary?

Is creation not an expression of God's spontaneous (*ungeschuldeten*) love?

Finally, the question about the meaning of life, as we like to put it today, also has its limits. No doubt, because of its ability to transcend the self man's life points beyond itself in spite of its contingency. But this fact should not lead to a new dualism between life as such and its meaning pointing towards something beyond itself. Human life actually gains by being related to something other and higher. Nevertheless, human life is always already meaningful in itself. It is therefore not wise to turn the question about the meaning into a general and fundamental question. It is better to limit it through an understanding of the justification and truth of existence. Otherwise the old moralism will easily exploit life in some new way.

The criticism of the question also turns to the implicit dichotomies which it contains or suggests. There is first of all the rift in that basic trust, the rift which puts the ball in God's court by asking: Why did you create me? Then there is the limitation of a question which concerns the whole of creation to that of the creation of 'man' or 'me'. There is also the segregation between man and this earth. The earth is only the present abode of man. The why and wherefore do not come into play here. Lastly, there is the separation between earth and heaven, or this world and the future world. This can be understood from the answer and should be criticised. But these distinctions are the expression of differences, a situation in which man finds himself, and which cannot be avoided. Yet if these differences reflect the misery which prompts the question about the meaning of life, they should not be fixed in the formulation of question and answer. But this would mean that the catechism answer should correct the question and in the end make it superfluous; it should not ratify it in what it asks and what it does not ask.

So it is necessary to explore the situation which causes the question to be asked in a particular way (Locher, Tracy). Every question is brought up for some reason or other. What, then, is the concrete situation which makes people really ask themselves: Why are we on this earth? and ask God: Why have you created me? The catechism puts the question in such an abstract way that one can think of a whole number of actual, physical and mental situations: suffering, guilt, loneliness, lack of a sense of direction, and so on. As the question is put it sounds like the metaphysical question: Why is something at all and not rather nothing? For what reason and by whom is man's life brought into the question about why, for what end, and meaning? Here the concrete and the general should be better combined than happens in the catechism. Theologically man's question about the meaning and purpose of his life must be causally linked with God's question about man as His likeness, the meaning and aim of His love. If man is not the answer to God's question, then God cannot be the answer to man's question.

Finally the relationship between being human and being a Christian remains unexplained and is therefore the subject of much criticism. The catechism question and answer only speak of the creative purpose and perfection of man's existence. Should this mean that being Christian is but a means towards the end of man's existence? Are we human in order to become Christian? Are we Christian in order to be truly human? Is being Christian in itself already a radical way of being human? Is being truly human already being unconsciously Christian? In practical terms: should a catechism begin with the general definition of being human or with the particular definition of being Christian? The articles of this issue show considerable tensions in the way these questions are answered.

CRITIQUE OF THE ANSWER

The contributions show more criticism than appreciation of the answer. The individual eschatology which it expresses is criticised throughout as too narrow and world-negating. Some asked that it should be filled out by bringing in the social dimension, cosmic universality and the Christian character of the purpose of life (Congar, Küng). Here a way seems to be open for a common consensus:

1. The meaning of individual human life can only be understood in the context of, not isolated from, the meaning of society, mankind and the cosmos. The quotations from Teilhard about the totalization of the world through the concentration of humanity at the end of time (Dobraczyński) and the visions (Cardenal) of a planetary revolution of freedom towards a classless humanity and the unification of the universe all point in this direction. But this still leaves open the question whether the traditional individual eschatology must be rejected as an individualistic kind of faith and an egotistic sense of salvation or whether it can be filled out by the perspectives of a social and universal eschatology, and how, finally, the future of salvation should be formulated if it is to embrace both man and the cosmos.

2. The future of salvation cannot be adequately understood if the answer to man's question is only given in purely theocentric terms. Almost all the contributions point to Christ as the ground for the understanding and reality of this future: communion with God comes about in and through communion with Christ, God's kingdom is present in the kingdom of Christ, man's likeness to God takes shape in conformity with Christ, which means: through sharing his death and his life (Mbiti). If this is so, then Christ cannot be understood merely as the 'means towards the end' of eternal happiness in God. The future of all-embracing salvation, opened up by Christ, must bear the mark of the Trinity.

3. Lastly, the answer to man's question about his meaning must bring divine and human activity together in a relationship which accords with the Gospel. 'To know God, to love him, to serve him and so to get into heaven' rather overstresses man's activity, makes God passive and insinuates that heaven is a reward for that activity. Is there then no meaning in suffering, loneliness and dying? And is the knowledge of God but a 'means to an end', so that we can get into heaven? Shouldn't the two-way process between the grace and bliss which God

bestows on us by allowing us to share in him, and the glorification which he receives from his creation through the Spirit be better conceived if we are to avoid contradictions (Schubert Ogden)?

The formulation of question and answer grew out of traditional Aristotelian metaphysics and the mystical tradition of the Middle Ages. A new formulation demands that the question be approached from (1) the Bible, and from (2) the point of view of the present state of society.

1. The question about the 'why of this life is answered in the Bible by the statement that we are meant to be 'like unto God'. The question about the meaning of life is answered by the *eschatological promise*. We get our cue from the divine promise which gives man a future and gives meaning to his life in the present.

The core of the eschatology of the Bible is certainly the *kingdom of God*. The kingdom of God is the core of Jesus' message. The coming of the kingdom and the call in its freedom are the substance of the messianic Gospel. Through Christ's surrender to death on the cross and his resurrection in the glory of God this kingdom was inaugurated among us. In his person and his history Christ is 'the kingdom of God among us'. This is why belonging to the kingdom of God is sharing his mission, his death and resurrection. This kingdom is first of all about God himself, his right over his creation, his union with his creation and his joy in the redeemed and united creation, and therefore his glorification (Bishop Antonic). But his glorification lies in the salvation of man, his likeness and image, and the peace of his creation, because it is the glorification of his self-giving, not self-interested, love. God's kingdom must therefore be thought of in terms of the beyond and of the here-and-now. It means a new creation for both earth and heaven. It embraces both the salvation of the soul and the redemption of the body, and with the liberation of man also the transfiguration of the cosmos (Garvey). When we see God's kingdom as the core of biblical eschatology we can justify the theocentric set-up of the answer given in the catechism. But we have of course not to explain God himself but God's kingdom as the goal and the meaningful future of man, if in the end we don't want to void creation of all meaning. In stating the purpose of everlasting happiness and the purpose of creation, we should avoid any gnostic-mystical revival of a return to some 'pan-unity'.

When God's kingdom is understood as the core of the answer to the question about the meaning and future of life, then it is also possible to bring individual eschatology and universal eschatology into the right relationship. The old answer only contained the individual eschatology because it pointed to God without his kingdom. Those new answers which are influenced by Marx, Nietzsche and Teilhard tend to the opposite one-sidedness in so far as they see the kingdom without God.

They might lead to the abandonment of all personal hope and the disso-
lution of the personality altogether for the sake of the liberation of
mankind and the consummation of the world: 'Instead of the beyond
above our grave in heaven we must put the beyond above our grave on
earth, the historical future, the future of mankind' (Feuerbach). When
we see God's kingdom as the core of our hope it is still possible to
speak of personal salvation, love and death, resurrection and eternal
life without egotism, since our egotism has been overcome by God's
glorification. Personal life and the assurance of personal meaning find
their rightful place in the true perspective.

In this view of God's kingdom the personal assurance is, however,
always an inclusive, never an exclusive one (Ching). It tends towards
all mankind and the whole creation because it is at one with God's
justice and God's love. The universality of hope bears the imprint of
the universality of the Creator and the Liberator of the world, and no
one else's. This is why this hope, centred on God's kingdom, reaches
beyond the boundaries of the personality, beyond the boundaries of the
Church, the peoples of mankind and human societies, right through to
nature itself. It reaches beyond the living to the dead and finds a future
for those that have gone before in the resurrection. It is precisely this
hope for the dead which shows that the universalism of God's kingdom
extends beyond all modern, earthly, present, evolutionary or revolutionary universalism.

Individual and social eschatology, human and cosmic eschatology
are intertwined in many ways. It remains, however, unsatisfactory to
express their mutual adjustment through mere addition ('not only—but
also'). Their interconnection seems to me to lie in the concept of man's
likeness to God. The question about the purpose of life must be answered by referring to life as it was meant to be. According to Genesis
1:26–8, man's likeness to God has four dimensions which cannot be
reduced to each other: the relationship with God, the relationship with
oneself, social relationship and relationship with the world. Any answer to the question: Why has God created man? must refer to the
community in these four dimensions. That man is intended to live in
accordance with God also distinguishes man from both God and the
rest of creation. According to the creation narratives creation proceeds
from matter to man as God's last work. According to the prophets and
the New Testament the order of redemption goes in the opposite direction: it begins with man's liberation and ends with the redemption of the
body, the liberation from servitude of all creation (Rom. 8) and the new
creation of heaven and earth at the end (Rev. 21). By virtue of this
likeness to God the individual eschatology cannot lose itself in the
social one nor the human eschatology in that of the cosmos however

much this likeness implies the individual's relation to the community and mankind's involvement with nature. Moreover, in virtue of the likeness to God mankind, reconciled through Christ and regenerated by the Spirit, has the task to reconcile, pacify and redeem nature, a task which it cannot abdicate. The universal tendency is one which goes out from man, particularly Christian man. Understood in any other way, it would lead man astray and dissolve the particular in the general.

2. As a matter of fact, we live in an age of growing unification and totalization. Science, technology and economics are, for the first time, bringing about the 'one world' and, with it, a 'common world history'. A manifold interdependence is weaving a whole net of political and social interrelationships which encompass the whole earth. This is precisely why segregation, divisiveness, enmity and oppression between groups of people, classes and nations as well as between societies and their natural environment must be considered as deadly. *The world for which all men are together responsible* is the task which confronts every man today. To fulfil this task it is essential to free the oppressed, to dismantle privilege and to democratize government. Christendom, too, must come out of its Europe-centred provincialism and enter the age of ecumenism. In the fight among religions and world-ideologies, and fully aware of this divided and oppressed world, it must give expression to the universalism of God's kingdom. For there lie the promise of history and the meaning of personal life. But it can only truly represent this hope in the name and through imitation of Christ. The Christological concentration and universalism of the kingdom seem to me to provide the right way of overcoming ecclesiastical wilfulness. The right of the individual, the right of the human community, and the right of nature can be worked out in such a way that it becomes possible to live together if we keep our eye on the justice of the coming kingdom of God.

Translated by Theo Weston

Contributors

ERNESTO CARDENAL is a world-famous Nicaraguan poet-priest and leader of a community on an island in Lake Nicaragua. His books range from epic poetry to contemplative and exegetical works conceived together with fellow members of his peasant community. Among English translations are: *Psalms/Psalms of Struggle and Liberation, The Gospel in Solentiname/Love in Practice, Marilyn Monroe and Other Poems*.

MAX CHARLESWORTH is Professor of Philosophy and Dean of the School of Humanities, Deakin University, Victoria, Australia, and editor of *Sophia*. Among his important published works are *Church, State and Conscience, The Problem of Religious Language* and *Philosophy of Religion: The Historic Approaches*. He was formerly a consultor to the Vatican Secretariat for Non-Believers.

JULIA CHING was born in China and converted to Catholicism in Hong Kong. She has taught at the Australian National University and at Columbia University, New York. She is now an associate professor at Yale University and among her major publications are *To Acquire Wisdom: The Way of Wang Yang-ming* and *Confucianism and Christianity*.

JAN DOBRACZYŃSKI has written over fifty novels, essays and historical sketches. His books have been translated into nineteen languages. He has received many Polish prizes. Translations into English are: *Letters of Nicodemus, To Drain the Sea, Sacred Sword* and *Hands on the Wall*.

JOHN GARVEY is a columnist for the U.S. journal *Commonweal* and writes for many other newspapers and journals. He is married, and an editor at Templegate Publishing Co., Springfield, Illinois, U.S.A.

Among his books are *A Contemporary Meditation on Saints* and *Saints for Confused Times*.

HANS KÜNG is one of the most famous of contemporary Catholic theologians. He is Professor of Dogmatic and Ecumenical Theology and Director of the Institute of Ecumenical Research at the University of Tübingen, Federal Germany. Among his best-known works are *The Church, Justification, Why Priests?, Infallible* and *On Being a Christian*.

GOTTFRIED LOCHER is Professor of Systematic Theology and History of Dogma at the Evangelical-Theological Faculty of the University of Berne, Switzerland. He is a member of the Presidium of the International Congress for Calvin Research and of many other important bodies. He has published major works on Zwingli, Calvin and Reformed theology.

JOHN MBITI is an Anglican priest currently working as Director of the Ecumenical Institute Bossey, Céligny, Switzerland. He was born in Kenya and has published many books and articles on religion and theology, for instance *New Testament Eschatology in an African Background, African Religions and Philosophy, Concepts of God in Africa* and *Love and Marriage in Africa*.

JÜRGEN MOLTMANN is a member of the Evangelical Reformed Church. He is has been Professor of Systematic Theology at the University of Bonn, Federal Germany, and is now Professor of Systematic Theology at the University of Tübingen in the same country. Among his best-known works are *The Theology of Hope* and *The Crucified God*.

SCHUBERT OGDEN is at present Professor of Theology and Director of the Graduate Programme in Religion at Southern Methodist University, Dallas, Texas, U.S.A. He is an ordained elder of the United Methodist Church. Among his best-known books are *Christ without Myth* and *The Reality of God and other Essays*.

PER ERIK PERSSON is Professor of Systematic Theology at the University of Lund, Sweden. He is a member of the Faith and Order Commission of the W.C.C., and among his major works are *Repraesentatio Christi* and *Sacra Doctrina: Reason and Revelation in Aquinas*.

ANTONIO PLAMADEALA is Bishop of Ploieşti, Romania. He is also Assistant Bishop to the Patriarch, Secretary of the Holy Synod of the Romanian Orthodox Church and Head of the Department for Foreign

Relations of that Church. He was Professor and Rector of the Faculty of Theology in Bucharest from 1971 to 1973. He is a member of the Executive Committee of the W.C.C. Among his major works are studies of the servant Church, Orthodox prayer and spirituality, and Hans Küng and the declaration *Mysterium Ecclesiae*.

FRANS VAN DE POEL has worked in catechetics for seventeen years, principally as editor of a major Dutch catechetical journal. He has published a number of books and articles on the teaching of religion. Since 1969 he has specialized in group dynamics in the Netherlands and in the U.S.A. He is now Supervisor at the Katholiek Pedagogisch Centrum as 's-Hertogenbosch, the Netherlands.

JACQUES-MARIE POHIER is a French priest and Professor at the Saulchoir Faculties, Paris, where he has been Vice-Rector for some years and Head of the Theology Faculty. Among his major publications are studies of psychology and theology and of the interrelations of theology and psychoanalysis.

DAVID TRACY is a priest of the Diocese of Bridgeport, Connecticut, U.S.A., and Professor of Philosophical Theology at the Divinity School of Chicago University. Among his major works are *The Achievement of Bernard Lonergan* and *Blessed Rage for Order: The New Pluralism in Theology*.